Succeed in Sales:

Effective Techniques to Be a Successful Salesperson

Introduction

In the dynamic and highly competitive world of sales, being a successful salesperson goes beyond simply knowing your product or service. It implies mastering a series of effective skills and strategies that will allow you to stand out in an increasingly demanding market. This book is presented as your complete guide to success in the field of sales, providing you with the necessary tools to become an outstanding salesperson.

You will learn the crucial importance of building strong relationships with your customers. You will understand how to build trust and loyalty through a personalized approach, tailoring your sales strategies to meet the individual needs of each customer. You will discover that empathy and active listening are essential to deeply understand the motivations and desires of your customers, which will allow you to generate a genuine connection with them.

Effective communication is another fundamental pillar that you will address in this book. You'll discover how to get your message across clearly and persuasively, using the power of words and nonverbal communication to positively influence your interactions with customers. You will learn to adapt your communication style to different personalities and buying styles, giving you a significant advantage in closing sales and building lasting relationships.

One of the most common challenges in sales is objections and rejection. This book will provide you with proven and effective techniques for overcoming objections constructively, turning them into opportunities to demonstrate the value of your offer. You will learn to handle rejection in a resilient way, using each experience as an opportunity to grow and improve your persuasion skills.

Ethics in sales is one aspect highlighted in this book. Emphasis is placed on the importance of maintaining high ethical standards in all of your business interactions. You will discover how to build relationships based on trust and transparency, avoiding misleading or manipulative practices.

Being an ethical seller will not only give you a solid reputation, but it will also allow you to build lasting and satisfying relationships with your customers.

This book will provide you with effective strategies to successfully close sales. You will discover how to use strategic questions to guide your customers towards an informed buying decision. You will learn to identify the needs and concerns of your customers and to present your offer as the ideal solution to satisfy them. The approach is based on creating value and helping your customers to visualize the benefits and results they will get by choosing your product or service.

This book offers a comprehensive and practical approach to becoming a successful salesperson. It will provide you with the skills necessary to build strong relationships, overcome objections, communicate effectively, and successfully close sales. If you're willing to commit and make the most of the insights shared in this valuable resource, you'll be one step closer to reaching new levels of success in your sales career.

About the Author

Walter Salt is a passionate writer and sales expert recognized for his work developing effective techniques for success in the world of sales. He was born and raised in Seattle, Washington, on the North American coast, where from an early age he demonstrated an interest in communication and persuasion.

After graduating with honors from the University of Washington, one of the region's leading educational institutions, with a Bachelor of Business Administration, Walter Salt began his career in the world of sales at one of the top 5 consumer goods companies. During her time at this prestigious company, she gained valuable experience in the field of sales, learning the intricacies of the sales process and developing effective techniques for building strong customer relationships.

Driven by his passion for writing and his desire to share his knowledge and experience, Walter Salt embarked on a career as a freelance writer. Over the years, he has written numerous articles, blogs, and materials related to sales and negotiation techniques, capturing the attention of a wide audience interested in improving their sales skills.

With his clear focus and ability to communicate complex ideas clearly and concisely, he has earned recognition in the sales community. In his constant search for knowledge and personal growth, Walter continues to research and update himself on the latest trends and techniques in the field of sales. In addition to his work as a writer, he also conducts seminars and trainings, sharing his valuable knowledge with sales professionals and ambitious entrepreneurs.

Throughout his career, he has shown his ability to adapt to different audiences and communication styles, establishing an authentic connection with his readers and followers. His dedication, results-oriented approach , and ability to build strong relationships have been key to his success as a writer and sales expert.

Walter Salt continues to inspire others with his passion for sales and his desire to help people reach their full potential in the field of sales. His unique combination of sales experience and effective writing skills make him an influential voice and trusted source for those looking to succeed in the exciting world of sales.

Chapter 1:
Know your Product or Service

In this chapter, you will learn the importance of having a deep understanding of the product or service you are selling. We will explore techniques to investigate and understand the details, features and benefits of the product, as well as its differentiation with respect to the competition. Plus, we'll teach you how to effectively communicate this information to your potential customers, thus creating a solid foundation for sales success.

The importance of knowing the product or service you are selling cannot be underestimated in the world of sales. In order to be a successful seller, it is crucial to have a deep and comprehensive understanding of what you are offering your customers.

When you understand your product or service in detail, you are able to convey trust and credibility to your customers. Having a mastery of its features, benefits, uses, and applications allows you to highlight its strengths and effectively respond to any questions or concerns that may arise during the sales process.

In addition, knowing your product or service in depth gives you the ability to highlight its differential value compared to the competition. You can clearly identify and communicate the competitive advantages it offers, which will allow you to persuade potential customers why they should choose it over other options available on the market.

Another benefit of having a thorough knowledge of the product or service is the ability to tailor it to the specific needs and desires of each customer. By understanding how your offer can meet their requirements and solve their problems, you can tailor your approach and make a compelling case that shows them how your product or service will directly benefit them.

Also, when you are knowledgeable about what you sell, you can anticipate and address potential objections or concerns that may arise from customers. This allows you to handle objections effectively and provide convincing responses that allay any doubts or uncertainties they may have.

Knowing the product or service you sell in depth is essential to being a successful seller. It gives you confidence, credibility and the ability to highlight the strengths and competitive advantages of your offer. In addition, it allows you to adapt to the needs of your customers, overcome objections and provide a personalized and compelling sales experience. So take the time to fully familiarize yourself with your product or service and become an expert at what you sell.

To know in depth the product or service you want to sell, you can follow the following steps:

1. Do Thorough Research –
Spend time researching and gathering information about the product or service. Use trustworthy sources such as the company's official website, promotional materials, market research, white papers, and any other relevant sources. Understand its operation, characteristics, benefits, uses, applications and any relevant details.

Let's imagine that the fictitious product we want to sell is a smart watch called " SmartTime ". To conduct a thorough investigation, we could follow these steps:

a) Official Website: We visited the official website of the company that makes the SmartTime . There we will find detailed information about the product, such as technical specifications, outstanding functions, design, materials used and compatibility with mobile devices. In addition, we will be able to obtain information about the company and its focus on technological innovation.

b) Promotional materials: We review the promotional materials provided by the company, such as brochures, catalogs or promotional videos. These materials can provide a visual description of the product and highlight key features and benefits such as fitness tracking, call and message notifications, music control, and more.

c) Market studies: We consult market studies related to smart watches and wearable devices in general. These studies can provide information on market trends, industry size, demand for similar products, and consumer preferences. We may also obtain data on competition and pricing strategies.

d) Technical Reports: We are looking for technical reports on the components and technologies used in the SmartTime . This may include details about the operating system, storage capacity, battery life, connectivity features (such as Bluetooth or Wi -Fi) and any other relevant technical specifications. These reports will allow us to understand the inner workings of the watch and its performance.

e) Reviews and Testimonials: We explore reviews and testimonials from users who have used the SmartTime . This will give us first-hand information about the user experience, customer satisfaction, and any problems or limitations that users have encountered. Reviews can also highlight features appreciated by customers and offer points of comparison with other similar products.

f) Online Forums and Communities: We participate in online forums and communities where smart watches are discussed. We can ask questions, interact with other tech enthusiasts, and get practical information about SmartTime . These communities are often great sources of additional information as users share their opinions, tips and tricks related to the product.

By conducting extensive research using these trusted sources, we will be able to fully understand the working, features, benefits, uses and applications of SmartTime . This will allow us to effectively present your strengths to customers, answer questions, and provide an informed buying experience.

2. Use the product or service :

The best way to fully understand what you are selling is to use the product yourself. Use the product or service in real situations to understand its usefulness and how it feels to use it. This will allow you to identify its strengths and limitations, as well as understand the needs it satisfies.

Continuing with our fictional product, the SmartTime , step 2 would involve using the smartwatch in real situations to experience it first hand. Let's see some examples of how we could do it:

a) Physical activity monitoring: We use SmartTime during our exercise routines to test its physical activity monitoring function. We record our steps, distance traveled, calories burned, and evaluate the accuracy of the data. We can also explore the heart rate monitoring and sleep analysis functions to understand how SmartTime can help improve our health and well-being.

b) Notifications and call management: We connect SmartTime to our mobile phone and use it to receive notifications of messages, emails or social networks. We tested the quick message display and reply functionality to assess its convenience and efficiency. In addition, we make and receive calls through the watch to check its audio quality and ease of use.

c) Music control: We use SmartTime to control music playback on our phone or on compatible devices. We evaluated the ability to navigate between songs, volume adjustment, and the convenience of having playback control right on our wrist. This allows us to understand how SmartTime can enhance our music experience while we are physically active or on the go.

d) Additional features: We explore the additional features of the SmartTime , such as GPS tracking, water resistance, downloadable apps, and customization options for faces and widgets. We use these features in real situations, such as outdoor sports or water activities, to test their performance and adaptability to different scenarios.

By using the fictitious product or service, SmartTime , in real situations, we can directly experience its features and functions. This allows us to identify the strengths of the smartwatch, such as its accuracy in tracking fitness or its comfort in controlling music, as well as helps us understand the limitations and how it adapts to different needs. By having this personal experience, we will be better prepared to communicate and demonstrate the benefits of SmartTime to potential customers.

3. Get trained and receive training:
Participate in training and education sessions provided by the company or manufacturer of the product or service. Take advantage of learning opportunities to acquire specific knowledge about its use, operation, maintenance and any relevant technical aspect.

Continuing our SmartTime example , Step 3 involves participating in training and education sessions provided by the smartwatch manufacturing company. Let's see how we could take advantage of these learning opportunities:

a) Initial Training: The company offers initial training for all SmartTime vendors . This session provides a detailed overview of the product, explains its key features and benefits, and offers guidance on how to effectively present it to customers. We learn about the differential value of SmartTime compared to other smartwatches and how to address common objections.

b) Technical training: The company organizes technical training sessions to deepen the operation of SmartTime . In these sessions, we are taught how to set up the watch, how to use all of its features, and how to troubleshoot basic technical issues that customers may face. We learn about firmware updates, how to perform a factory reset, and how to fix connectivity issues.

c) Hands-On Sales Sessions: The company provides opportunities to participate in hands-on sales sessions where interactions with real customers are simulated. In these sessions, we are given feedback on our presentation, communication skills, and ability to highlight the strengths of SmartTime . We learn to adapt our approach according to the needs and preferences of each client and how to close sales effectively.

d) Online Training Resources: The company provides online training resources, such as how-to videos and detailed manuals, which allow us to delve into different aspects of SmartTime . These resources cover topics such as advanced feature usage, tips and tricks to maximize the user experience, and specific use cases for different customer segments. We learn how to use SmartTime optimally and answer frequently asked questions from customers.

e) Participation in conferences and events: The company invites its vendors to participate in conferences and events related to the smartwatch industry and wearable technology. These opportunities allow us to learn from experts in the field, learn about the latest trends and technological advances, and connect with other industry professionals. We learn from the experiences shared by other sellers and stay up to date on the market landscape.

By participating in training and education sessions, we gain specific knowledge on the use, operation and maintenance of SmartTime . This allows us to be well-prepared to answer technical customer questions, provide expert advice, and demonstrate confidence in the product. Being well trained, we can convey credibility and security to customers, which increases our chances of success in SmartTime sales .

4. Connect with experts:
Seek the expertise of people who are already familiar with the product or service. You can contact colleagues, mentors or company representatives to obtain additional information, answer questions and take advantage of their experience. Take advantage of networking opportunities to make valuable connections with experts in the field.

Continuing with the SmartTime example , step 4 involves seeking the experience of people who are already familiar with the smartwatch. Let's see how we could connect with experts in the field:

a) Fellow sellers: We reach out to colleagues who also sell the SmartTime to get additional information and share experiences. We can ask them about successful sales strategies, how they have addressed common customer objections, and how they have highlighted the key features and benefits of SmartTime . Exchanging ideas with colleagues can provide us with new perspectives and approaches.

b) In-company mentors: If the company has a mentoring program, we approach an experienced mentor in sales of similar products or specifically SmartTime . We can schedule regular meetings to discuss our doubts, receive personalized advice and learn from the mentor's experience. Mentors can give us valuable advice on how to improve our sales skills and how to deal with specific challenges.

c) Company representatives: We contact the representatives of the company that manufactures the SmartTime to obtain additional information and resolve specific questions about the product. Representatives can provide us with technical details, product updates, and recommendations on best selling practices. We use their experience and knowledge to better understand SmartTime and how to position it in the market.

d) Industry Events: We attend wearable technology and smartwatch industry events. There, we look for opportunities to make valuable connections with experts in the field, such as industry leaders, product developers, and other vendors. We participate in talks, round tables and networking activities to learn from their experiences, share knowledge and establish lasting relationships.

e) Online Groups and Communities: We join online groups and communities related to smartwatches and wearable technology. These groups give us the opportunity to interact with experts, ask questions, share information, and learn from the collective knowledge. We actively participate in discussions, ask questions, and offer our own expertise to build valuable relationships with experts in the field.

By connecting with experts in the field of SmartTime , we can benefit from their experience and knowledge. These connections help us answer questions, obtain additional information, learn from successful strategies and obtain valuable advice to improve our sales skills. Leveraging the expertise of experts gives us a competitive advantage by providing a more informed and valuable service to clients.

5. Participate in demos and events:
If possible, attend demos or events related to the product or service. There you will be able to witness its operation live, ask questions directly to the experts and learn from the experiences shared by other sellers or users. This will give you a practical and enriching perspective.

Continuing our SmartTime example , Step 5 involves participating in smartwatch-related demos and events. Let's see how we could take advantage of these opportunities:

a) SmartTime are shown live . We attend these demos to witness how the watch interacts with mobile devices, how settings are made, and how its key features are used. During the demo, we can ask questions directly to the experts to clarify any doubts and obtain additional information about SmartTime .

b) wearable technology and smart watches. At these events, companies showcase their products and services, including SmartTime . We take the opportunity to interact with company representatives, get hands-on experience with SmartTime , and get up-to-date information on the latest trends and developments in the industry. We also connect with other sellers and users to learn from their experiences and share knowledge.

c) Launch Events: If your company hosts a launch event to introduce a new version or update to SmartTime , we attend to be the first to know what's new. At these events, detailed information on product enhancements and new features is provided. We can watch live demos, ask the experts questions, and get an exclusive look at the future of SmartTime . This allows us to stay current and ready to promote the latest innovations.

d) Webinars and Online Conferences: We participate in webinars and online conferences on wearable technology and sales. These events allow us to learn from experts in the field and hear experiences shared by other vendors. Topics like effective sales strategies, tips for promoting tech products, and best practices in the smartwatch industry can be covered. Through these platforms, we can ask questions, interact with other participants and expand our knowledge about SmartTime .

e) User sessions: The company organizes user sessions where sellers and users of SmartTime share their experiences and knowledge. We participate in these sessions to hear real use cases, learn about users' favorite features, and understand how SmartTime has positively impacted their lives. These sessions provide us with an enriching and hands-on perspective on the product, which helps us connect more effectively with customers and convey the actual use experience.

Participating in demonstrations and events related to SmartTime allows us to have a practical and enriching experience of the product. By witnessing it live, asking questions directly of the experts, and learning from experiences shared by other vendors and users, we can improve our understanding of SmartTime and more effectively communicate its benefits to customers. Also, these opportunities keep us up to date on the latest news and trends in the smartwatch industry.

6. Stay updated:

Knowledge about the product or service should not be static. Stay up to date with news, updates and improvements related to it. Follow company news, participate in refresher courses, and stay informed about trends and developments in your industry. This will allow you to maintain up-to-date and relevant knowledge.

Step 6, staying current, is crucial to being a successful marketer. Let's see how we can apply it with examples:

a) Company news monitoring: We regularly monitor news and communications from the company that manufactures the product or service we sell. We subscribe to your newsletter, follow your social networks and visit your official website. This allows us to keep abreast of product updates, important announcements, events and special promotions. For example, if the company releases a new version of the product or introduces an innovative feature, we make sure we understand the details and how it impacts the advantages and benefits we can offer to customers.

b) Participation in refresher courses: We enroll in refresher courses and professional development related to the product or service. These courses can be provided by the manufacturing company, educational institutions, or online platforms. For example, if we sell a business management software application, we make sure to participate in courses that keep us up to date on the latest trends in the field of business management and best practices in using the application. This helps us to keep knowledge up to date and relevant, enabling us to offer better advice and support to customers.

c) Industry Research: We stay informed on trends and developments in our industry. We read relevant blogs, articles, research and studies. We participate in discussions in forums and online groups where topics related to our product or service are discussed. For example, if we sell home security devices, we keep abreast of the latest innovations in the field of security, such as the use of artificial intelligence and the integration of IoT devices . This allows us to offer our clients up-to-date information and recommend solutions that meet their current needs and expectations.

d) Participation in Industry Events: We attend conferences, trade shows, and industry events related to our product or service. These events give us the opportunity to learn from experts in the field, listen to talks and presentations on relevant topics, and network with other professionals. For example, if we sell medical equipment, we attend medical conferences where advances in medical technology are presented and new treatments are discussed. This helps us keep abreast of developments in our industry and keep abreast of our customers' changing needs and expectations.

e) Interaction with Clients and Colleagues: We maintain active communication with our clients and colleagues to obtain feedback and stay abreast of changing market needs. We listen to customers' suggestions and feedback about the product or service and the trends they are seeing in their industry. We also share information and experiences with colleagues to keep abreast of best practices and learn from their successes and challenges. This interaction provides us with valuable information that helps us keep our knowledge up to date and adapt our sales strategy accordingly.

Remember that the process of getting to know a product or service in depth is continuous and requires constant dedication. The more involved and immersed you are in the topic, the more confidence and skill you will gain to sell it effectively.

There are various techniques that can be used to investigate and understand the details, features and benefits of a product, as well as to identify its differentiation from the competition. We will explore some of these techniques below:

1. Market analysis:
Market analysis is an essential technique to fully understand the environment in which a product or service operates. It consists of carrying out an exhaustive study that involves the collection and analysis

of data related to competitors, the target audience, market trends and customer segments. This analysis provides an overview of the competitive landscape and helps identify how the product is positioned compared to others.

By analyzing the market, it is possible to detect niches or customer segments that are not being adequately served by the competition. This opens the door to the identification of business opportunities and the creation of unique value propositions that satisfy those unmet needs.

The seller can carry out a thorough investigation of the market in which it operates to identify niches or customer segments that are not being adequately served by the competition. This involves collecting demographic data, conducting trend analysis, studying consumer behavior, and analyzing the strengths and weaknesses of competitors. The hygienic plate brand conducts extensive market research and discovers that there is a customer segment that is looking for high-quality, affordable disposable plates for outdoor events such as barbecues in the park. Note that the current competition does not offer disposable options with hygienic and resistant characteristics. You must be attentive to the needs and desires of customers. This involves actively listening to customers, conducting surveys, conducting interviews, and gathering feedback to better understand what problems they are facing and what solutions they want. By identifying unmet needs, the seller can develop unique value propositions that meet those needs.

The brand conducts surveys and interviews with potential customers and finds that many care about hygiene and comfort when using disposable plates at outdoor events. Customers want dishes that are strong, biodegradable, and won't warp easily with hot foods or sauces.

The successful seller must keep abreast of the strategies and actions of the competition. Observing how competitors are approaching the market and which customer segments they are neglecting can reveal business opportunities. The seller can find ways to differentiate itself from the competition by offering something unique and valuable to those underserved segments. The brand researches the competition and notes that most disposable plate brands focus on convenience and affordability, but don't pay much attention to hygiene and strength.

This creates an opportunity to offer high-quality, hygienic dishes that meet unmet customer needs.

Staying abreast of emerging industry trends can give the seller a competitive advantage. Identifying new technologies, changes in consumer preferences, government regulations, or any other factors that may influence the marketplace can create opportunities to adapt or develop products and services to meet those emerging demands. The brand realizes that more and more people are concerned about the environmental impact of disposable products. Taking advantage of this trend, they decided to develop compostable hygienic dishes made with biodegradable and environmentally friendly materials. This allows them to differentiate themselves from the competition and serve an environmentally conscious customer segment.

You can benefit from collaborating with other professionals within the organization or in the industry as a whole. By sharing knowledge and experiences, new perspectives and market opportunities can be discovered that might otherwise go unnoticed. The brand partners with experts in biodegradable and sustainable materials to develop hygienic dishes that meet quality standards and are resistant to heat and sauces. By collaborating with these professionals, the brand manages to improve the formula of its dishes and offer a unique solution on the market.

Identifying market opportunities involves a strategic approach that combines market research, competitor analysis, understanding customer needs, and observing market trends. By identifying uncovered niches and creating unique value propositions, the seller can take advantage of these opportunities and generate significant business success and growth.

2. Personalize the sales approach:
Market analysis provides information on customer preferences and characteristics. By better understanding consumers, marketers can tailor their sales approach, messaging, and storylines to more effectively connect with their target audience. For example, if a customer segment is identified as particularly valuing sustainability, the seller may highlight the green features of the product to appeal to that specific group.

The seller should use demographic and market data collected during market analysis to identify customer segments that particularly value sustainability. This data may include information about the age, geographic location, level of education, and purchasing preferences of consumers. Having identified the customer segment interested in sustainability, the salesperson can tailor their sales message to highlight the green features of the product. This involves highlighting how the fictional hygienic dish product is made from biodegradable, recyclable, or sustainably sourced materials. You can also highlight the environmental benefits of choosing these dishes, such as the reduction of plastic waste or the positive impact on the environment.

The vendor should develop a customized sales pitch that highlights how the hygienic dish product aligns with the specific values and concerns of the customer segment interested in sustainability. You can focus on reducing the use of single-use plastic, promoting the circular economy or contributing to environmental conservation. To support their sales pitch, the seller can use relevant examples and testimonials from other satisfied customers who also value sustainability. This can include stories from customers who have chosen hygienic dishes and experienced the environmental benefits, as well as testimonials from experts or recognized institutions endorsing the quality and sustainable approach of the product.

In addition to highlighting the sustainability of the product, the successful marketer can offer customized solutions that are tailored to the specific needs of customers interested in sustainability. This can include shipping options with sustainable packaging, recommendations for responsible use of the product or even special discounts for customers committed to protecting the environment.

By customizing the sales approach and adapting to customer preferences and characteristics, the successful salesperson can more effectively connect with the customer segment interested in sustainability. By highlighting the green features of the product, tailoring the sales message, using relevant testimonials, and offering personalized solutions, the salesperson can influence customers' buying decisions and achieve greater effectiveness in their sales efforts.

3. Differentiate yourself from the competition:

Through market analysis, you can identify how the product or service is positioned compared to the competition. This helps the seller to highlight the unique features, benefits, and competitive advantages that the product offers. By highlighting the differences and clearly communicating why the product is superior or more appropriate, customers can be persuaded to choose it over available alternatives.

The seller must perform a thorough analysis of the market to understand how the product or service is positioned in comparison to the competition. This involves identifying direct and indirect competitors, researching their sales strategies, analyzing their strengths and weaknesses, and understanding how the product or service is perceived in the marketplace. Using a Straight Razor for example, the razor brand conducts a thorough analysis of the market and discovers that there is a lack of high-quality razor options aimed at the male market that values both shaving performance and product aesthetics. It identifies that the competition focuses mainly on functionality and does not pay much attention to design and style.

The seller must identify the features and benefits of the product or service that make it unique compared to the competition. This can include things like superior quality, increased durability, innovative design features, a specific focus on sustainability, or any other distinctive features that provide additional value to the customer. The seller identifies that it can set itself apart by offering razors with high-quality stainless steel blades that provide a precise and smooth shave. In addition, it highlights that its razors have an elegant and modern design, which makes them a style accessory that men can wear with pride.

Once the unique features and benefits have been identified, the seller must clearly communicate the value proposition of the product or service. This involves highlighting how you differentiate yourself from the competition and how you uniquely benefit customers. The salesperson can emphasize the specific aspects that satisfy the needs and desires of the customer, highlighting the tangible and emotional results that are obtained when choosing the product or service. Seller clearly communicates that their product stands out in the marketplace by combining exceptional shaving performance with sophisticated design. It highlights how your razor provides a close shave, minimizes skin irritation, and offers optimal control and precision. In addition, it stands out that its elegant and ergonomic design allows a comfortable and pleasant shaving experience.

The seller may use demonstrations, practical examples, or testimonials from satisfied customers to support the competitive advantages of the product or service. This can help build customer trust and credibility by showing how the product or service has generated positive results for other customers in similar situations. In addition, you can directly compare features, benefits, and competitive advantages with competing products or services to highlight their superiority. The salesperson shows customers how his stainless steel razor stays sharper longer compared to other options on the market, resulting in a smoother, longer-lasting shave. Additionally, it features testimonials from satisfied customers highlighting how the brand's razor has significantly improved their shaving experience and helped them achieve a more polished and sophisticated look.

To further differentiate themselves from the competition, the successful salesperson must provide excellent customer service. This means being available to answer questions, provide personalized advice, offer quick solutions to problems and ensure an overall positive shopping experience. Exceptional customer service can be a competitive advantage in itself, as customers value the care and support they receive before, during, and after the purchase. Seller is committed to exceptional customer service by offering personalized advice on razor selection and care. He makes sure customers feel supported at every stage, from product selection to post-purchase follow-up. In addition, they offer satisfaction guarantees to demonstrate the confidence they have in the quality and performance of their razors.

By analyzing the market, identifying unique features and benefits, communicating the value proposition, demonstrating competitive advantages, and offering excellent customer service, the successful salesperson can differentiate themselves from the competition and highlight the distinctive qualities of the product or service. This helps to capture the attention of customers, build trust and achieve a strong position in the market.

4. Identify trends and changes in the market:

Market analysis also makes it possible to identify emerging trends and changes in consumer preferences. This gives sellers the opportunity to stay on top of the latest trends and adapt their sales strategy accordingly. For example, if a shift in preferences toward healthier products is observed, the seller may focus on highlighting the health benefits of their product.

The seller must be constantly updated on the latest trends and changes in the market. This involves reading trade publications, following thought leaders on social media, participating in relevant conferences and events, and networking in the industry. Being aware of the news and changes in the market is essential to identify opportunities and adapt the sales strategy accordingly. As a technology vendor, it's important that you stay up to date on the latest trends and developments in the industry by following leading companies like Apple, Google, and Microsoft. By learning what's new in products and technologies, the seller can tailor their sales approach and highlight the unique features of the devices they offer to their customers. As a fashion retailer, it's critical to stay on top of the latest trends by following influential brands like Gucci, Louis Vuitton, and Zara. This allows you to offer personalized advice to your customers, suggesting styles and garment combinations that are on-trend and in line with their individual style.

The seller must closely observe the competition to identify the strategies and tactics they are implementing in response to market trends. This may involve analyzing their online presence, following their posts and communications, and keeping track of any new products or services they are launching. Understanding how the competition is adapting their sales strategy provides valuable insights into the opportunities and challenges present in the marketplace. In your role as a smartphone seller, it is important that the seller is constantly watching how brands like Samsung adapt to market trends and launch new models. This allows you to stay on top of competitor pricing strategies, features, and promotions, helping you position and highlight the unique benefits of the devices you represent. In your position as a health food vendor, you need to keep a close eye on the Whole Store food Market to understand how they respond to changing consumer demands. This allows you to offer innovative products and solutions to your customers who are looking for healthier and more sustainable options.

Customers are an invaluable source of information on the latest trends and changes in the market. The seller must be attentive to the comments, questions and needs expressed by customers. Conducting surveys, conducting interviews, or having open conversations with customers can help identify emerging trends and changing market demands. This information can be used to adapt the sales strategy and offer solutions that meet the current needs of customers. Working as a seller in a coffee shop, it is important for the seller to listen carefully to the preferences and requests of his customers. If many of them express an interest in non-dairy options, you can suggest almond milk or soy milk alternatives. This shows that you are committed to meeting their needs and providing them with a personalized experience. As a seller on an eCommerce platform, it's crucial to keep an eye on customer reviews and feedback on products. If multiple customers express a need for additional functionality in a product, the vendor can communicate this to the development team so they can consider implementing that enhancement.

A successful salesperson must have the ability to quickly adapt to trends and changes in the marketplace. This implies being agile and flexible in the planning and execution of the sales strategy. If a new trend or change in the market is identified, the salesperson must be willing to adjust their sales approaches, messages, and tactics to take advantage of the opportunities that arise. This may involve developing new products or services, adopting new sales technologies, or implementing innovative marketing strategies. In your role as a streaming services vendor , it's important to stay on top of content consumption trends and how they evolve. This allows you to tailor your sales approach and highlight features like autoplay to the next episode that aligns with how customers enjoy your content. As a vendor in the urban mobility industry, you need to keep up to date with new transportation options emerging, such as electric scooter and bike rental services . This allows you to offer personalized mobility solutions to your customers based on their needs and preferences.

The successful salesperson must constantly be evaluating the performance of their sales strategy and adjusting it accordingly. This involves analyzing the results, measuring the success of the implemented tactics and making changes when necessary. If a trend or change in the market is not generating the expected results, the seller must be willing to adapt their approach and try new strategies to stay relevant and competitive. Working as a beverage vendor, it's critical to constantly assess customer response to different products and flavors. If you see increased demand for low-calorie, sugar-free options, you can adjust your sales strategy and highlight those options to meet your needs.

By staying informed, monitoring the competition, listening to the customer, being agile and flexible, and constantly evaluating and adjusting the sales strategy, the successful salesperson can identify trends and changes in the marketplace and adapt their sales approach accordingly. This allows you to capitalize on emerging opportunities and stay relevant in an ever-evolving business environment.

Market analysis is an essential tool for sellers as it provides them with valuable information about competitors, target audience and market trends. By applying this technique, salespeople can identify opportunities, personalize their sales approach, differentiate themselves from the competition, and adapt to changes in the marketplace. This allows them to make more informed decisions and develop more effective strategies to achieve success in their sales work.

Ketel Sellers One

In the 1990s, Ketel One was a relatively unknown vodka in the United States, and its presence in New York bars was limited. However, the owners of the Ketel distillery One , the Nolet brothers , were determined to change that and make their vodka a recognized brand in the industry.

Rather than take a conventional approach to marketing and advertising, the Nolet brothers decided to focus on building relationships with bartenders and bar owners in New York. They knew that if they could win the endorsement of cocktail experts, Ketel vodka One would become a popular choice among consumers.

They began by personally visiting the city's bars and restaurants, introducing themselves to the bartenders and sharing their family history and the dedication they put into creating their vodka. They were offered samples of Ketel vodka One and invited them to try it and experiment with it in the creation of cocktails.

The strategy turned out to be effective. Bartenders were impressed by the quality and smoothness of Ketel vodka One , as well as for the authenticity and passion of the Nolet brothers . They began recommending it to their clients and including it in their cocktail menus. Word spread quickly through the New York bartending community, and Ketel vodka One began to gain popularity in the bars of the city. Soon, consumers also began to ask for it in other bars and establishments.

The strategy of building relationships with bartenders and gaining their trust was key to Ketel 's success. One in New York. As more and more bartenders became ambassadors for vodka, organic demand was created among consumers. Ketel brand One was associated with quality, authenticity and the endorsement of the bartending community , which contributed to its growth and recognition in the spirits industry.

The history of Ketel vodka One in the Bars of New York demonstrates the importance of building strong, authentic relationships with key professionals in the industry. By earning the trust and endorsement of bartenders , a brand can become recognized and appreciated by consumers, fueling its success and growth in the marketplace.

Chapter 2:

Active listening

1. The importance of Active Listening

Active listening is an essential skill that every successful salesperson must master. In the competitive world of sales, it's not just about talking and persuading, it's about understanding and connecting with customers in a meaningful way. It is the basis for building strong and lasting relationships with customers. It goes beyond just hearing the words the customer says. It is about paying attention and fully concentrating on what they are expressing, both verbally and non-verbally.

When we practice active listening, we strive to understand the meaning behind the client's words. This involves reading body language, gestures, facial expressions, and other nonverbal cues that can reveal additional information.

For example, a customer may say, "I need a phone with a long battery life." If we only stick with those words, we could suggest a phone with a high capacity battery. However, when applying active listening, we can notice that the customer also shows frustration when mentioning this, which could indicate that they have had previous experiences with short battery life phones. In this case, we would understand that your need is not only to have a long battery life, but to avoid the frustration of running out of battery during the day.

Active listening allows us to capture the client's needs, desires and concerns accurately and deeply. By being fully present in the conversation, we are able to identify the subtleties and nuances in your speech, giving us a fuller understanding of your expectations and requirements. In addition, it fosters empathy towards the client. By putting yourself in their shoes and understanding their perspectives, we can make a more authentic and genuine connection. This contributes to strengthening the relationship with the client and builds trust, since they feel that we are committed to understanding and satisfying their needs.

Active listening allows us to go beyond superficial words and understand the deep meaning behind them. By accurately capturing customer needs, wants and concerns, we are able to provide personalized solutions and build strong, lasting relationships. It is a fundamental skill for successful salespeople as it allows us to provide quality service and exceed customer expectations. Show respect to the customer and show that you value their opinion. By showing genuine interest in what they have to say, customers feel heard and understood, creating an environment of mutual trust.

Active listening involves not only understanding what the client is expressing directly, but also reading between the lines and capturing the true needs that may be implicit in their communication. This ability to uncover subtle clues and understand unspoken needs is extremely valuable to successful salespeople.

By paying attention to detail during a customer interaction, you can spot verbal and nonverbal cues that reveal hidden needs and desires. For example, a customer may mention that they need a high-quality product, but may also show interest in learning about the durability and warranty characteristics of the product. These signals indicate that durability and reliability are critical to the customer, and tailoring our solutions based on this information allows us to deliver products that exactly match what they are looking for.

In addition, active listening gives us the opportunity to deepen our understanding of the client by asking open-ended and exploratory questions. These questions allow us to learn more about your specific needs, preferences and circumstances. For example, by asking, "What is most important to you when choosing this type of product?" we can uncover key aspects such as budget, convenience, or aesthetics that are critical to effectively meeting customer needs. .

This valuable information that we obtain through active listening allows us to adapt our solutions and offer products or services that fit exactly what the client is looking for. By understanding your deep needs, we can provide personalized recommendations and offer specific benefits and features that solve your challenges and deliver real value.

Active listening gives us a competitive advantage by gaining valuable insight into customer needs and wants, even those they may not express directly. By paying attention to detail, reading between the lines, and asking the right questions, we can tailor our solutions and deliver products or services that exactly fit what they're looking for. This strengthens our position as sellers and allows us to provide a personalized and satisfying customer experience. Asking clear and relevant questions is a crucial active listening skill. These questions are designed to elicit more detailed and specific information about the client's needs, wants, and concerns. By asking open-ended questions, meaningful dialogue is encouraged and the client is invited to express their opinions and expectations in greater depth.

By asking the right questions, significant benefits are generated. In the first place, it allows obtaining a more complete and precise vision of the client's needs. By deepening our understanding of your situation, challenges and goals, we can provide more relevant and personalized solutions. This allows us to offer products or services that fit exactly what the customer is looking for, generating greater satisfaction and loyalty.

Also, asking pertinent questions demonstrates a genuine interest in the customer and their needs. This helps establish a stronger connection and strengthens the business relationship. The client feels valued and understood, which creates an environment of mutual trust. As this trust is built, the client will be more inclined to share relevant information and seek our guidance in decision-making.

The meaningful dialogue generated through active listening and asking pertinent questions also makes it easier to build long-term business relationships. It lays the groundwork for ongoing collaboration and open communication between the vendor and the customer. By understanding and addressing changing customer needs over time, we are able to adapt our offerings and stay aligned with your ongoing expectations. This promotes a relationship of trust and long-term loyalty, which in turn can generate referrals and additional sales opportunities.

In short, successful salespeople recognize that active listening involves asking clear, relevant questions to deepen their understanding of customer needs. Doing so creates a meaningful dialogue that establishes a stronger connection and makes it easier to build long-term business relationships. Active listening and pertinent questions are powerful tools that allow us to better understand the client, provide personalized solutions and maintain successful business relationships over time.

2. Benefits of active listening in the sales process:

a) **Understanding customer needs:**
By practicing active listening, the salesperson can capture the customer's needs, wants, and concerns accurately and deeply. This allows you to tailor your sales approach and offer solutions that fit exactly what the customer is looking for. By understanding the customer's needs, the salesperson can provide more relevant recommendations and increase the chances of closing the sale.

b) **Build trust and empathy** :
Active listening shows the customer that the closer is genuinely interested in their situation and in understanding their perspectives. By paying attention and showing empathy, the closer creates an environment of trust and connection with the customer. This facilitates open communication and makes the client feel more comfortable expressing their needs and concerns. As trust builds, the customer will be more willing to consider the seller's recommendations and establish a long-term business relationship.

c) **Identify Upsell Opportunities** :
Through active listening, the salesperson can identify cross-sell or upsell opportunities. By understanding customer needs and carefully listening to feedback, the salesperson can identify areas where additional products or services can further complement or satisfy customer needs. This not only benefits the customer by providing more complete solutions, but also generates additional sales opportunities for the seller.

d) **Overcome Objections and Resolve Problems** :
By actively listening to customer concerns and objections, the

closer can effectively address them. By understanding the reasoning behind these objections, the salesperson can offer personalized responses and solutions that allay customer concerns and help them make an informed buying decision. This shows the customer that the seller is committed to resolving their concerns and providing quality service.

e) ***Get valuable feedback:***
Active listening also allows the salesperson to gather valuable feedback about their products, services, and sales process. By listening to customer feedback and suggestions, the salesperson can identify areas for improvement and make adjustments to their sales approach. This feedback is essential for the salesperson's professional growth and development, as it gives them the opportunity to improve their performance and deliver an even better customer experience in the future.

Active listening provides numerous benefits to the salesperson in the sales process. From understanding customer needs and building trust, to identifying upsell opportunities and solving problems, active listening is an invaluable tool for salesperson success. By practicing this skill, the salesperson can improve their ability to provide personalized solutions, build lasting relationships, and achieve results that are satisfying for both the customer and themselves.

3. Development of active listening skills .

Developing the skill of active listening is critical for any salesperson who wants to improve their performance and build strong customer relationships.

The skill of active listening can be developed by practicing it in everyday life. Pay active attention to conversations with friends, family, or colleagues. Make a conscious effort to listen carefully and fully understand what you are being told. This will help you transfer and apply this skill in your business interactions. It requires being present in the moment and paying full attention to the customer. Practicing mindfulness in everyday life can help develop this skill. Take time each day to focus on the present and actively observe your surroundings, your thoughts, and your physical sensations. This will help you train your mind to be more present and focused during customer interactions.

During customer interactions, it's important to eliminate distractions and spend time solely listening. Turn off or silence your phone, avoid looking in other directions, and focus fully on the customer. This shows the customer that you value their time and are dedicated to listening. Reflective listening involves repeating or paraphrasing the key ideas that the client has expressed. This not only shows the customer that you have understood their message, but also allows you to confirm your understanding and clear up any misunderstandings. Practice reflective listening by repeating or summarizing what the client has said to show that you are actively listening and understanding their needs.
Asking open-ended questions encourages deeper and more detailed communication with the client. These questions invite the client to share more information and to express their thoughts and feelings more fully. Practice asking open-ended questions that start with words like "How?", "What?", "Why?" to promote a richer and more meaningful dialogue. Taking notes during the customer interaction is an effective way to show that you are engaged and value their information. This helps you remember important details and shows the customer that you are taking their needs into account.

Empathy is essential in active listening. Strive to put yourself in the customer's shoes and understand their emotions, perspectives, and needs. Show empathy through gestures, facial expressions, and comments that reflect your understanding and support for the customer.

Remember that developing the skill of active listening requires practice and perseverance. Over time, by applying these strategies consistently, you can improve your ability to listen actively and provide a more satisfying experience for your customers.

4. Techniques to improve active listening.

There are several techniques that can be learned from the world's great salespeople to improve active listening. Here are some practical examples:

a) **Reflect and paraphrase:**
    This technique consists of repeating or summarizing the main ideas of the client to demonstrate that it has been understood correctly. An example of this is the famous car salesman, Joe Girard, who was noted for repeating the customer's needs and wants during the sales conversation. By reflecting and paraphrasing, the closer shows the customer that they are paying attention and care to understand their needs.

b) **Follow-up questions:**
    Great salespeople use follow-up questions to deepen their understanding of customer needs and concerns. For example, Mary Kay Ash, founder of Mary Kay Cosmetics , used to ask open-ended questions like "Could you tell me more about that?" or "How do you think this could affect your business?" These questions allow the salesperson to obtain more information and better understand the customer's situation.

c) **Strategic silence:**
    Strategic silence is a powerful technique used by many great salespeople. It consists of remaining silent after the client has made a statement or expressed a concern, giving the client an opportunity to expand or deepen their thinking. This technique can also be used to give the client time to reflect or make a decision. For example, Grant Cardone , a well-known salesperson and author, uses strategic silence to allow the customer to think and feel more comfortable sharing more information.

d) **Nonverbal Active Listening:**
    Great salespeople understand the importance of paying attention to the customer's gestures and body language. For example, Tony Robbins, a famous motivator and salesperson, has stressed the importance of observing a customer's eye movements and facial gestures for clues about their preferences and emotions. Nonverbal active listening complements verbal active listening and helps the salesperson better understand the customer's needs and wants.

e) **Summarize and recap:**
    At the end of a customer conversation or interaction, great

salespeople often summarize and recap the key points discussed. This technique allows the closer to demonstrate that they have actively listened and understood the information provided by the customer. By summarizing and recapitulating, the closer also gives the customer an opportunity to correct any misunderstandings or add additional information. For example, Zig A well-known author and motivational speaker, Ziglar used to summarize the client's needs and goals at the end of the conversation to make sure they were both on the same page.

These are just some of the active listening techniques that can be learned from the world's great salespeople. Each of them has developed their own style and approach, but they all share the ability to listen carefully and understand the client's needs. By studying and learning from their techniques, salespeople can improve their skills.

5. The art of asking effective questions to understand customer needs.

The art of asking effective questions in the context of understanding customer needs involves the ability to ask strategic questions that reveal insightful and relevant information. We can liken this skill to the art of asking questions in movies, where filmmakers use carefully crafted questions to develop the plot and reveal the truth about the characters.

Some examples of how we can define the art of asking effective questions, using cinematographic references, are the following:

a) *"The Key Question":* In many movies, there is a central question that triggers the development of the story. Similarly, in the art of effective questioning, there is a key question that can reveal the customer's true need. For example, in the movie "The Curious Case of Benjamin Button ", the key question could be: "What do you really want in life?" The salesperson must develop the skill of identifying the key question that will reveal the customer's true need. Uncovering the customer's motives and goals behind their purchase will allow the seller to tailor their approach and offer customized solutions that meet those specific needs.

b) ***"The Surprise Question":*** Just like in the movies, where surprise questions can change characters' perspective and reveal important information, in sales, asking unexpected questions can reveal hidden customer needs. For example, in the movie "The Origin", the surprise question would be: "If you could have anything in the world, without limitations, what would it be?" By asking unexpected questions, the closer can capture the customer's attention and uncover hidden needs or unspoken desires. These pop questions can help spark a deeper and more meaningful conversation, allowing the salesperson to better understand the customer's motivations and offer relevant solutions.

c) ***"The Revealing Question":*** In some movies, there are revealing questions that help the characters understand themselves and make important decisions. In sales, asking insightful questions can help the salesperson understand the customer's deeper motivations and needs. For example, in the movie " Lost in Translation ", the revealing question would be: "What really makes you happy in your job?". The closer should use revealing questions that help the customer reflect on his current situation and his future goals. These questions allow the salesperson to better understand the customer's deepest needs and wants, which in turn makes it easier to present products or services that are aligned with those needs and wants.

d) " ***The Dare Question":*** Movies sometimes feature challenge questions that force the characters to reflect on their situation and make difficult decisions. In sales, asking challenging questions can lead the customer to reconsider their options and discover new needs. For example, in the movie "Fight Club", the challenge question would be: "If you were not afraid of failure, what would you like to achieve in your professional life?" Challenge questions allow the closer to lead the customer to question their beliefs and consider new possibilities. By asking challenging questions, the closer can help the customer explore alternatives and discover solutions they might not have previously considered. This involves asking questions that encourage the client to reflect and make more informed decisions.

By applying these effective questioning techniques, salespeople can improve their active listening skills, better understand customer needs, and offer relevant, personalized solutions. This, in turn, helps build strong customer relationships, build trust, and increase the chances of sales success.

6. Importance of paying attention to detail during interactions with customers.

The importance of paying attention to detail during interactions with customers lies in the ability to capture relevant information and better understand their needs and preferences. By paying attention to detail, salespeople demonstrate a genuine commitment to the customer, which strengthens the relationship and increases the chances of sales success.

When salespeople pay attention to detail during customer interactions, they can pick up on verbal and nonverbal cues that give them valuable information. This includes observing the client's body language, capturing facial emotions and expressions, as well as paying attention to subtle comments or indicators of interest. These details can help sellers tailor their sales approach, personalize their recommendations, and provide more relevant solutions.

Additionally, by paying attention to detail, salespeople show respect and consideration for the customer. This creates a more positive and memorable customer experience, which can build long-term loyalty. Customers feel valued when a salesperson shows genuine interest in their needs and takes the time to understand their specific situation.

An example of the importance of paying attention to detail in real life is personalized service in a restaurant. When a waiter pays attention to detail while interacting with diners, they may note their food preferences, allergies, or dietary restrictions. This allows the waiter to offer appropriate recommendations and customize the service based on the individual needs of each customer. The customer feels valued and cared for, which improves their experience in the restaurant and increases the possibility that they will return in the future.

Paying attention to detail during customer interactions is critical to understanding customer needs, tailoring your sales approach, and delivering personalized service. Successful salespeople understand that small details can make a difference in the customer experience and build strong, long-term relationships.

7. The ability to read between the lines and capture the underlying concerns of customers.

Reading between the lines goes beyond the words customers say and focuses on understanding needs and concerns that may not be apparent to the naked eye. This skill allows the salesperson to identify hidden customer concerns and offer solutions that effectively address those concerns.

When a salesperson can read between the lines, they can detect indirect cues, tone of voice, body language, and other subtle aspects that reveal the customer's underlying concerns. These concerns may be related to budget, product quality, durability, previous customer satisfaction, or any other factor influencing your decision making.

By capturing these underlying concerns, the salesperson can proactively address them and offer solutions that reassure the customer and build trust. This involves presenting specific features or benefits that address concerns and demonstrating how the product or service can effectively meet your needs.

An example of the importance of reading between the lines and capturing the underlying concerns of customers is the success of a life insurance salesperson. Suppose a customer is interested in purchasing life insurance, but during the conversation, the salesperson perceives some insecurity and concern about whether his family would be well cared for in the event of his death.
Sensing the customer's insecurity and concern about his family's financial protection in the event of his death, the salesperson adopts a reassurance-oriented, empathetic approach. Instead of focusing solely on

product features, it focuses on specific benefits that directly address the customer's concern.

The seller uses examples of real cases where life insurance has provided financial security to families in difficult situations. You can tell stories of people who, thanks to their life insurance policy, managed to keep their loved ones financially stable after a tragic event. By doing so, the salesperson not only demonstrates their understanding of the client's concerns, but also provides concrete evidence of how life insurance can make a difference in difficult times.

This personalized, concern-based approach builds trust and establishes an emotional connection between salesperson and customer. The client feels heard, understood and supported in their concerns. As a result, you are more likely to trust the seller's recommendations and be willing to purchase life insurance to protect your family. By addressing these underlying concerns and demonstrating a genuine understanding of the client's concerns, the salesperson will build trust and increase the chances of success in the life insurance sale. This focus on the customer's concerns will be the ultimate key to the seller's success.

The ability to read between the lines and capture underlying customer concerns allows salespeople to tailor their approach, address concerns, and offer solutions that meet customer needs. This skill is critical to establishing a strong connection, building trust, and achieving sales success.

8. How to use active listening to customize solutions that meet the individual needs of each client.

Active listening is a powerful tool that successful salespeople use to tailor solutions to meet the individual needs of each customer. By being responsive and paying attention to detail during customer interactions, salespeople can capture key information that allows them to tailor their products or services to meet each person's specific needs.

By using active listening, salespeople can identify the unique needs of each customer and fully understand their wants, preferences, and challenges. This involves going beyond superficial responses and exploring more deeply the client's motivations and goals. By asking relevant questions and observing verbal and nonverbal cues, salespeople can gain valuable insight into customer preferences, expectations, and concerns.

Once sellers have collected this information, they can use it to customize solutions that perfectly fit each customer's individual needs. For example, if a customer is looking for business management software, the salesperson can use active listening to understand the specific challenges the customer is facing in their industry. You can then recommend software that effectively addresses those challenges and provide concrete examples of how it has helped other customers in similar situations.

The customization of solutions based on active listening shows the client that the seller cares about understanding their needs and finding the best option for them. This creates a bond of trust and shows the customer that the seller is committed to providing exceptional service tailored to their specific situation.

Additionally, by customizing solutions, vendors can stand out from the competition and add differential value. Clients appreciate when they are provided with a tailored solution that addresses their specific needs and helps them achieve their goals. This not only leads to increased customer satisfaction, but also to long-term business relationships and positive word-of-mouth recommendations.

Using active listening in the sales process allows salespeople to understand each customer's individual needs and customize solutions that precisely meet those needs. This not only improves the customer experience, but also establishes a relationship of trust and generates positive results for both sellers and customers.

Case studies and practical examples of how active listening has led to sales success.

Case Study: Apple Store

Apple is a renowned technology company headquartered in Cupertino, California. Founded in 1976, Apple has become one of the industry's foremost leaders, known for its innovation in products like the iPhone, iPad, Mac, and Apple Watch , as well as its ecosystem of software and services.

Apple sets itself apart with its focus on sleek design, build quality, and user experience. The company has established strong brand loyalty and has a globally diverse customer base.

In terms of estimated annual sales, Apple has experienced significant growth over the years. According to the company's financial reports, in fiscal 2020, Apple generated total revenue of approximately $274.5 billion. However, it is important to note that sales figures may vary from year to year due to factors such as market demand, new product introductions, and competition in the technology industry.

Case in point: At Apple stores, employees are known for their focus on active listening. During a visit to an Apple Store, a customer expressed interest in an iPhone, but also mentioned his passion for photography and the need for a high-quality camera. The employee, using active listening, recommended the iPhone with advanced photo features and shared examples of photos taken with the device. By tailoring the solution to customer needs and preferences, Apple was able to close a successful sale and create a positive customer experience.

In this case study, Apple employees' focus on active listening was instrumental in delivering a successful and personalized customer experience. During the in-store interaction, the clerk not only took note of the customer's interest in an iPhone, but also paid attention to his mention of photography and the need for a high-quality camera.

Active listening allowed the employee to understand the customer's specific needs and find the right solution. Rather than simply offering the latest iPhone or the most popular model, the employee used his knowledge of the iPhone's advanced photography features to highlight how the product could satisfy the customer's passion for photography.

In addition, by sharing examples of photos taken with the device, the employee provided tangible proof of the quality and performance of the iPhone's camera. This helped the customer to visualize how the product could meet their expectations and exceed their needs.

The ability to tailor the solution to individual customer needs and preferences, thanks to active listening, enabled Apple to close a successful sale. Additionally, the customer experienced a sense of added value by receiving a personalized recommendation and seeing how the product aligned with their interests and passions.

This Apple Store case study shows how active listening can lead to sales success by enabling sellers to deeply understand customer needs and deliver personalized solutions that build satisfaction and trust.

Case study: Zappos

Zappos is a renowned e-commerce company specializing in the sale of footwear and accessories. Founded in 1999, it has been noted for its focus on providing an excellent customer service experience. Zappos is known for its wide selection of products, hassle-free return policies, and a highly-trained customer service team.

In terms of estimated annual sales, based on data through 2021, Zappos generated about $1.3 billion in annual revenue. This figure has fluctuated over the years, but it has positioned Zappos as one of the top companies in the footwear e-commerce industry.

In addition to its focus on customer satisfaction, Zappos has also been noted for its unique company culture. The company strives to create a positive work environment and encourage creativity and innovation among its employees. Zappos has been recognized for its people-centered approach and commitment to excellence in customer service.

Practical example: Zappos , the renowned online shoe store , has made active listening one of its main pillars of customer service. An example of his approach is when a customer calls to return a shoe. Instead of simply processing the return, Zappos agents take the opportunity to listen carefully to the customer and discover their preferences, likes and needs.

Based on this information, agents offer personalized recommendations for other products that might be of interest to the customer. This practice of active listening has contributed to Zappos' success and exceptional reputation for customer service .

In the case study of Zappos , the online shoe store, active listening has been critical to its success and reputation for customer service. When a customer calls to return a shoe, Zappos agents don't just process the return mechanically. Instead, they take this opportunity to practice active listening and better understand the customer.

Zappos agents take the time to listen carefully to the customer, paying attention to their preferences, likes and needs. They can inquire about the reason for the return, the customer's expectations, and what features they are looking for in a pair of shoes. This information is key to fully understanding the customer and personalizing the shopping experience.

Zappos agents take the opportunity to offer personalized recommendations for other products that might be of interest to the customer. For example, if the customer mentions that they are looking for comfortable athletic shoes, agents might suggest additional options from popular brands and models that fit those specific needs. This practice of active listening and offering personalized recommendations creates additional value for the client, since they feel understood and cared for individually.

Active listening at Zappos has contributed greatly to its exceptional reputation for customer service. Customers feel valued and appreciated when their needs are understood and they are offered a personalized shopping experience. This practice has led to high levels of customer satisfaction and increased brand loyalty. Additionally, the positive word of mouth generated by these experiences has been a key factor in Zappos ' continued growth and success in the footwear e-commerce industry.

Zappos ' active listening approach during customer interactions, including in return cases, has proven to be an effective strategy for improving the customer experience and building brand loyalty.

By understanding and serving the individual needs of each customer, Zappos has set an exemplary standard in customer service and has established itself as a leader in the e-commerce industry.

Case study: Starbucks

Starbucks is a renowned international chain of coffee shops and one of the most iconic brands in the coffee industry. Founded in 1971 in Seattle, United States, Starbucks has expanded globally with thousands of stores around the world.

The company has stood out for its focus on coffee quality, customer experience and creating a welcoming atmosphere in its establishments. Offers a wide variety of coffee drinks, teas, cold drinks, bakery items, and prepared food options.

Starbucks has managed to establish a strong presence in various international markets, gaining recognition and loyalty from consumers. Its estimated annual sales in fiscal 2021 were approximately $28.5 billion, highlighting its position as one of the leaders in the coffee industry.

The company has also made a commitment to sustainability and has implemented initiatives to promote responsible practices in the coffee supply chain, as well as to reduce its environmental impact.

Starbucks has become a globally recognized brand, known for its focus on coffee quality, customer experience, and its presence in diverse markets. Its success is reflected in its significant annual sales and its commitment to sustainability.

Case in point: Starbucks has been known for its focus on active listening to create personalized experiences for its customers. During a visit to a Starbucks store, a barista noticed a customer mentioning a preference for drinks with less sugar and more healthy options. The barista used active listening to offer low-sugar drink alternatives and lactose-free or dairy-free milk options. By responding to customer needs and preferences in a personalized way, Starbucks was able to deliver an exceptional experience and build customer loyalty.

In the case of Starbucks, active listening has become a fundamental part of its culture of customer service. Baristas are trained to pay attention to detail and capture customers' needs and preferences during their interactions. A practical example of this is when a customer mentions their preference for drinks with less sugar and healthy options.

In this case, the barista demonstrates active listening skills by being attentive to the customer's request and understanding their desire for healthier alternatives. Using his knowledge of the Starbucks menu, the barista can recommend low-sugar beverages, such as coffee options with no added sugar or sweetened with natural sweeteners. In addition, the barista may offer lactose-free or dairy-free milk options for those customers with specific dietary needs.

By responding to customer needs and preferences in a personalized way, Starbucks manages to deliver an exceptional experience. The customer feels valued and understood, which strengthens the emotional connection with the brand. This personalized attention not only creates a positive experience in the moment, but also contributes to long-term customer loyalty. The customer becomes a brand advocate and is more likely to come back and recommend Starbucks to others.

This case study highlights how active listening at Starbucks goes beyond just taking orders. Baristas strive to understand each customer's individual preferences and needs and offer personalized solutions. This not only drives the company's success, but also contributes to its reputation as a place where customers feel heard and cared for.

These real cases demonstrate how active listening has been key to the success of renowned brands such as Apple, Zappos and Starbucks. By paying attention to customer needs and preferences, these companies have been able to build strong relationships, increase customer satisfaction, and foster brand loyalty.

10. Final advice and recommendations to develop and maintain active listening skills in the field of sales.

1. Practice Mindfulness: Cultivate the ability to be present in the moment and pay complete attention to customer interactions.
2. Eliminate distractions: Avoid distractions such as mobile phones or irrelevant thoughts during conversations with customers.
3. Avoid interrupting: Allow clients to express themselves fully before intervening. Avoid interrupting them or finishing their sentences.
4. Ask open-ended questions: Use open-ended questions to encourage a deeper conversation and obtain relevant information.
5. Pay attention to non-verbal cues: Observe the customer's body language, facial expressions and tone of voice to pick up additional information.
6. Repeat and paraphrase: Summarize and repeat what the customer has said to make sure you correctly understand their message.
7. Show empathy: Put yourself in the customer's shoes and show understanding and empathy towards their needs and concerns.
8. Be patient: Do not rush to answer. Give the client the time they need to fully express themselves.
9. Use silence: Sometimes silence can allow the client to reflect and share additional information.
10. Take notes: Keep a record of the key points mentioned by the client for future reference and to show your interest in their message.
11. Practice active listening outside of work: Apply active listening in your daily interactions outside of work to develop and strengthen the skill.
12. Seek feedback: Ask your colleagues or supervisors for feedback on your active listening skills and look for areas of improvement.
13. Learn from others: Observe successful salespeople and take note of their active listening techniques to incorporate into your own style.

14. Participate in personal development courses: Consider the possibility of attending communication and active listening courses to learn new techniques and strategies.
15. Reflect and analyze: After each interaction with a customer, take a moment to reflect on your performance and look for opportunities to improve your active listening skills.

Remember that active listening is a skill that requires practice and continuous effort. The more you dedicate to developing it, the better results you will obtain in your sales and customer relations.

The Beer Seller

Jaime was a talented salesperson who worked for a well-known beer company. He was known for his ability to practice active listening and understand the needs of his clients.

On one occasion, Jaime visited a potential client named Roberto, who owns a local bar and restaurant. Roberto was looking to add a new beer to his menu, but was having a hard time finding an option that would really stand out and appeal to his customers.

Instead of immediately presenting the features and benefits of his beers, Jaime decided to use the technique of active listening. He asked open-ended questions so that Roberto could express his wishes and expectations regarding the beer he wanted to offer.

Jaime listened attentively to Roberto's answers, showing a genuine interest in his preferences and needs. He asked follow-up questions to deepen his understanding and discovered that Roberto was looking for a unique and distinctive beer that would delight his customers and set his establishment apart from the competition.

With all the information he had collected, Jaime was able to offer a customized solution. He recommended a locally produced craft beer, with innovative flavors and an attractive presentation. He explained how this beer would capture the attention of customers and create a unique experience at Roberto's bar.

In addition to the beer recommendation, Jaime shared tips on food pairings and how to promote beer to increase demand. He demonstrated extensive knowledge of the brewing industry and offered practical suggestions to boost sales and customer satisfaction.

Jaime's ability to practice active listening and adapt to Roberto's needs was appreciated. Roberto appreciated the fact that Jaime took the time to listen to him and understand his vision, which was reflected in his decision to include the recommended beer on his menu.

This story illustrates how active listening can make a difference in sales, even in the context of selling beer. By listening and understanding customer preferences and needs, salespeople can offer personalized solutions and build a genuine connection. Active listening not only leads to successful sales, but also builds strong, long-lasting relationships with customers.

Chapter 3:
Establishing Lasting Relationships

Building strong customer relationships is essential to long-term sales success. In this chapter, we'll explore strategies for making meaningful connections with your customers, from first contact to after-sales. You'll learn how to build trust, how to adapt to different communication styles, and how to stay in touch with your customers to strengthen relationships and generate repeat sales opportunities.

1. Importance of lasting relationships in sales:

The importance of lasting relationships in sales is that customers are not only looking to purchase a product or service, but also to establish a meaningful connection with the brand and feel valued. Here are reasons why building and maintaining strong customer relationships is critical to long-term sales success:

A. Customer loyalty:

By building lasting relationships, the bond between the customer and the brand is strengthened, leading to greater loyalty. Satisfied and engaged customers are more likely to repeat purchases and recommend the brand to others, which translates into continued business growth.

Building lasting and meaningful customer relationships strengthens the bond between the customer and the brand, which in turn generates greater customer loyalty. When customers are satisfied and engaged, they are more likely to repeat purchases and recommend the brand to others, which translates to continued business growth. It is essential to build trust. By building strong relationships, salespeople create an environment in which customers trust their knowledge and the quality of the products or services they offer. Customers who trust a vendor are more willing to continue doing business with them and to recommend them to others.

In addition to trust, customer loyalty implies repeat purchases. By getting to know customers and understanding their needs and preferences, sellers can offer customized solutions that fit their requirements. This personalization in the sales process creates a positive experience for the customer, increasing the chances that they will make purchases again with the same seller instead of looking for alternatives in the market. Customer loyalty is essential to a vendor's long-term success. By building lasting relationships, building trust, and offering personalized solutions, sellers can cultivate customer loyalty. This not only translates into repeat purchases, but also referrals and referrals that help expand your customer base and ensure continued business growth.

B. Increased customer retention:

When you build a strong relationship with customers, you reduce the likelihood that they will switch to the competition. The trust and loyalty that is built through a long-term relationship gives customers less reason to look for alternatives, and they feel more secure in continuing to do business with the same brand.

When a seller manages to establish a solid relationship with its customers, the probability that they will switch to the competition is significantly reduced. The trust and loyalty that is built through a long-term relationship gives customers less reason to look for alternatives, and they feel more secure in continuing to do business with the same brand.

Let's imagine a salesperson for a telecommunications company who has built a strong relationship with one of their customers over several years. This solid relationship has been built through various actions and behaviors on the part of the seller, which have generated trust and loyalty in the client. First, the seller has demonstrated their commitment to providing excellent customer service. You have been constantly available, whether through phone calls, emails or personal visits. Whenever the client has had a concern or problem, the seller has responded quickly and efficiently, showing a proactive and decisive attitude.

In addition, the seller has established open and transparent communication with the customer. You have been receptive to listening to customer needs and concerns, showing empathy and understanding. Through active listening, he has been able to understand the client's expectations and has worked together to find adequate solutions to their requirements.

The seller has also maintained regular communication with the customer, even after the initial sale. You have been following up regularly to ensure that the customer is satisfied with the service and to be aware of any changes in their needs. This continued attention has strengthened the relationship and built trust in the company and the vendor as a trusted long-term partner.

Imagine a clothing store salesperson who has been known for her commitment to getting to know her customers on an individual basis. This salesperson understands that each customer is unique and has different preferences and needs. Therefore, he takes the time to establish a personal connection with each one of them.

The salesperson initiates conversations with customers, either during their in-store visit or through online interactions, to better understand their tastes, lifestyle, and clothing-buying goals. Use active listening to capture the details and preferences that customers bring up during these conversations.

In addition, the salesperson asks pertinent and clear questions to deepen the understanding of each customer's individual needs. For example, you can ask about the occasion they're looking for clothes for, their favorite colors, the brands or styles they're attracted to, and any other relevant information that helps them provide personalized recommendations.

By taking the time to get to know their customers on an individual basis, the salesperson builds a relationship of trust and shows that they genuinely care about meeting their needs. This personalized approach allows the seller to provide accurate and relevant recommendations to each customer, resulting in a unique and satisfying shopping experience.

Customers value the attention and care that the seller puts into their shopping experience. They feel understood and appreciated, which strengthens the relationship between the seller and the customer. As a result, these customers are motivated to return to the store again and again, confident that they will receive exceptional service and recommendations tailored to their tastes and needs.

When a salesperson takes the time to get to know their customers on an individual basis, they build a trusting relationship and provide personalized recommendations, creating a memorable shopping experience and building customer loyalty.

C. Increase in cross and upsells:

By gaining a deep understanding of customer needs and preferences, it is possible to identify opportunities to offer complementary products or services. A long-lasting relationship allows for a better understanding of changing customer needs, which naturally leads to upselling and cross-selling.

By gaining a deep understanding of customer needs and preferences, a salesperson has the opportunity to identify opportunities to offer complementary products or services. Through a long-standing relationship and ongoing dialogue with the customer, the salesperson can gain a better understanding of the customer's changing needs, enabling him or her to present additional solutions that are relevant and beneficial.

When a salesperson understands a customer's specific needs, they can suggest additional products or services to complement their initial purchase. For example, if a customer purchases a camera, the seller may offer additional lenses, a carrying bag, or a tripod that are compatible with the camera. This upsell not only increases the value of the sale, but also meets the broader needs of the customer and enhances their experience.

In addition to upselling, a salesperson can take advantage of a long-standing relationship to encourage cross-selling. This implies offering products or services related to but different from those that the customer has previously purchased. For example, if a customer has purchased a mobile phone, the salesperson might suggest accessories such as wireless headphones, a protective case, or a portable charger. These cross-sells take advantage of the seller's knowledge of the customer's interests and preferences, providing additional options that can enhance the customer experience and fill additional needs.

The key to success in increasing cross- and up-sells lies in the salesperson's ability to actively listen to the customer, understand their needs and preferences, and present relevant and personalized solutions. By establishing a lasting relationship with the customer, the seller has the opportunity to continue meeting their needs over time, adapting to their changes and offering complementary products or services that enrich their experience.

"Upsale " strategy in their day-to-day activities in various ways. You can offer add-ons or accessories that enhance the experience of the main product. You can also recommend related products that are of interest to the customer. Another option is to present higher versions of the product with additional features or higher quality. In addition, you can offer packages or special promotions that include several products or services at a more advantageous price.

This concept of "upsale " refers to the practice of offering a customer the purchase of additional or higher value products or services during a transaction. It is about persuading the customer to purchase an additional item or service that complements their initial purchase, thus increasing the total value of the sale.

upsale " strategy is McDonald's. When placing an order at the counter, McDonald's employees often ask if the customer would like to add large fries or a larger soft drink for a small price increase. In this way, the company promotes an additional sale and increases the value of the transaction. Another example is when they offer the option of adding extra toppings to the burgers, such as additional bacon or cheese, for an additional cost.

The objective of the "upsale " is to increase the average sales ticket and generate more income by offering products or services that complement the customer's initial purchase. To achieve this, it seeks to identify opportunities during the sales process to offer additional options that may be attractive to the customer and improve their experience.

It is important to emphasize that the "upsale " must be carried out in an ethical manner and for the benefit of the client. It is about offering relevant and valuable options that adjust to the customer's needs and preferences, giving them the opportunity to improve their purchase and obtain a more satisfactory experience.

The long-term relationship with the customer allows the salesperson to identify opportunities to increase cross-sell and up-sell. By gaining a deep understanding of the customer's needs and preferences, the seller can offer complementary products or services that meet those needs and enrich the customer experience. This not only increases the value of the sale, but also strengthens the customer relationship in the long term.

D. *Valuable Feedback:*

By establishing a strong relationship with clients, an open environment of communication and trust is fostered, allowing for honest and constructive feedback. This feedback is invaluable for improving products, services and sales processes, which in turn strengthens the relationship with customers.

The concept of valuable feedback refers to the benefit of establishing a strong relationship with customers, which creates an environment conducive to receiving honest and constructive feedback. This feedback is critical to the growth and continuous improvement of a business, as it provides key information about how products, services, and sales processes are perceived from the customer's perspective.

When a relationship based on trust and openness is established, customers feel comfortable expressing their opinions and sharing their experiences. The successful salesperson takes this opportunity to receive valuable feedback that they can use to make adjustments and improvements to their offer.

Valuable feedback provides insight into what is working well and what could be improved. Customers can offer suggestions, highlight positive aspects, and also raise concerns or areas for improvement. By receiving this feedback in an open and responsive manner, the salesperson demonstrates their commitment to customer satisfaction and their willingness to adapt and evolve based on their needs.

This feedback can have a significant impact on the development and refinement of products, services, and sales processes. It can help identify opportunities for improvement, correct potential deficiencies, and adapt to changing market trends. By implementing changes suggested by customers, the salesperson shows a willingness to listen and respond to their needs, thus strengthening the relationship and fostering customer loyalty.

An example of the importance of valuable feedback is a software company developing a new mobile app. As they release the app to the market, they engage in active communication with users and solicit their feedback. Users provide feedback on ease of use, functionality, and features they would like to see in future updates.

Based on this valuable feedback, the company can make improvements to the app, fixing bugs, optimizing the user interface, and adding new features that meet the needs of users. This attention to customer feedback not only improves product quality, but also strengthens the relationship between the company and its customers, building long-term trust and loyalty.

An example of a well-known vehicle brand that has used valuable customer feedback to improve its products and strengthen customer relationships is Tesla. Tesla is known for its focus on innovation and customer satisfaction.

Tesla has used feedback from its customers to make significant improvements to its electric vehicles. Through surveys, online forums, and direct communication with Tesla owners, the company collects information about the driving experience, desired features, and any issues or issues that may arise.

Based on this valuable feedback, Tesla has made software updates to fix bugs, improve performance, and add new features to its vehicles. In addition, they have implemented improvements in the charging infrastructure and in the network of charging stations, responding to the needs and comments of their customers.

This focus on customer feedback has proven effective for Tesla, as it has allowed it to improve the quality and performance of its vehicles, meeting the needs and expectations of its customers. Continuous attention to customer feedback has helped strengthen the relationship between Tesla and its customers, building trust and long-term loyalty.

From a salesperson's point of view, valuable customer feedback can be a powerful tool for improving sales and strengthening customer relationships.

When a salesperson receives feedback from customers about the products or services they offer, they have the opportunity to better understand the needs and expectations of the market. This feedback can provide key information about the strengths and weaknesses of the products, as well as ideas for possible improvements.

By using this valuable feedback, the salesperson can tailor their sales approach and pitches to highlight the features and benefits that customers value. For example, if a customer mentions that they would like an additional feature in the product, the salesperson can highlight how the current product meets other needs while also mentioning that an update is in the works that will include the requested feature. This shows the customer that their feedback is valued and that you are working to meet their long-term needs.

In addition, by demonstrating that customer feedback is heard and taken into account, the salesperson can establish a relationship of trust and credibility. Customers will feel valued and will be more willing to continue interacting with the seller, which can lead to long-term business relationships.

An example of how a salesperson can use valuable feedback is in car sales. If a salesperson receives frequent feedback from customers about the lack of a certain safety system in a particular car model, they may communicate that information to the manufacturer. In turn, the manufacturer can take steps to improve the vehicle and add that safety system in future versions. The seller can use this updated information when interacting with customers, highlighting improvements, and providing reassurance to potential buyers.

From a salesperson's point of view, valuable customer feedback is a valuable tool for improving sales and strengthening business relationships. By listening and responding to feedback, the salesperson can tailor their sales approach, highlight features and benefits that customers value, and establish a trusting relationship. This can lead to increased customer satisfaction and long-lasting business relationships.

E. Competitive Advantage:

Maintaining lasting relationships with customers creates a sustainable competitive advantage. Competitors may try to attract customers with lower prices or promotions, but the relationship and trust built over time makes customers more resistant to competitive efforts and more likely to continue choosing the brand.

The ability to maintain long-lasting relationships with customers provides a significant competitive advantage to a brand. Although competitors may try to attract customers through strategies such as lower prices or promotions, the relationship and trust built over time make customers more resistant to competitive efforts and more likely to continue choosing the brand. . A successful salesperson understands that sales success is not just about closing a transaction, but about building strong, long-lasting relationships with customers. You understand that maintaining a loyal and satisfied customer base is a key competitive advantage in today's marketplace.

When a brand manages to establish a strong relationship with its customers, an emotional bond and a sense of loyalty are created. Customers feel valued and appreciated, which strengthens their connection to the brand and builds long-term preference. As the relationship develops, a level of mutual trust is established, making customers less likely to seek alternatives and more inclined to continue to trust the brand. Establishing and maintaining lasting customer relationships offers multiple benefits. First, a satisfied and loyal customer is more likely to make repeat purchases and recommend the brand to others, leading to a steady stream of business. Furthermore, by maintaining a close relationship with customers, the seller can better understand their changing needs and adapt their offers and recommendations accordingly.

This sustainable competitive advantage is based on several factors. First of all, the brand understands the individual needs and preferences of each client, which allows it to offer personalized solutions and effectively meet their specific demands. By actively listening and maintaining constant communication, the brand can adapt to changes in customer needs and expectations, further strengthening the relationship.

Additionally, the brand invests in creating positive customer experiences. This means providing excellent customer service, exceeding expectations, and adding value to every interaction. These positive experiences generate positive emotions and strengthen the relationship with the customer, making it difficult for the competition to separate customers from the brand. The successful salesperson understands that building lasting relationships is based on trust and customer satisfaction. This means providing excellent customer service, being available to answer questions and resolve issues, and treating each customer as an individual. By doing so, the salesperson establishes a positive reputation and becomes a trusted advisor to their customers.

A practical example of this competitive advantage can be seen in the mobile phone industry. Many brands have managed to maintain lasting relationships with their customers by offering loyalty programs, exclusive benefits and excellent customer service. Even though there are competitors with similar offerings, customers continue to choose the brand with which they have developed a strong and trusted relationship. Even if there are more attractive offers on the market, the relationship and trust built over time make customers less likely to switch providers.

Maintaining lasting relationships with customers creates a sustainable competitive advantage for a brand. The relationship and trust built over time make customers more resistant to competitive efforts and more likely to continue choosing the brand. By understanding individual customer needs, offering personalized solutions, and delivering positive experiences, a brand can strengthen its position in the marketplace and maintain a lasting competitive advantage.

In addition, the successful salesperson recognizes that maintaining long-term customer relationships creates a barrier to entry for the competition. Although other competitors may offer lower prices or attractive promotions, the relationship and trust built over time make customers less likely to seek alternatives. The successful seller knows that customer loyalty is not based only on price, but on the quality of service and personalized attention offered.

The competitive advantage of maintaining long-term customer relationships is vital to your long-term success. The vendor focuses on providing exceptional service, understanding the individual needs of each customer, and establishing a relationship built on trust and satisfaction. By doing so, the seller positions itself as a trusted and preferred partner in the marketplace, generating a steady stream of business and making it harder for the competition to separate customers from the brand.

2. Building trust:

Building trust is a crucial element in the sales process. Here are the three key stages to building trust with customers:

A. First contact:

The first contact with the customer is a crucial opportunity to establish a good impression and build trust. At this early stage, there are several key strategies a seller can employ to achieve this.

One of the fundamental strategies is to be honest and transparent from the beginning. Avoiding exaggerations or false promises is essential to building a relationship based on trust. If there are limitations or features that are not available in the product or service offered, it is important to clearly communicate this to the customer. This initial transparency demonstrates integrity and establishes a solid foundation for trust.

In addition, it is important to show empathy towards the client's needs and show a genuine interest in their well-being. By actively listening to the customer and understanding their concerns, the salesperson can tailor their approach and offer tailored solutions. This personalized attention shows the customer that the seller is committed to their satisfaction and builds trust in the relationship.

Following through on promises and commitments made during first contact is another key strategy for building trust. If the seller agrees to provide additional information, send samples, or provide specific follow-up, it is essential to deliver on these promises in a timely manner. This shows the customer that the closer is serious about their relationship and their needs, and demonstrates trustworthiness.

Finally, providing excellent customer service is essential during the first contact. This involves responding in a timely manner to customer inquiries or requests, providing clear and accurate information, and demonstrating knowledge and competence in the area. If a customer has specific questions about the product, the salesperson must be able to answer accurately and demonstrate their expertise on the subject. This level of customer service conveys professionalism and confidence.

During the first contact with the customer, a successful salesperson focuses on establishing a good impression and building trust. This is accomplished by being honest and transparent, demonstrating empathy, and showing a genuine interest in the client's needs. In addition, fulfilling promises and commitments, as well as providing excellent customer service, are fundamental actions to establish a solid relationship based on trust from the beginning. These key examples illustrate how a salesperson can apply these strategies in their interaction with customers.

B. Developing the relationship:

The seller must ensure that all promises and commitments made during the sales process are met. For example, if a product has been agreed to be delivered by a specific date, the seller must ensure that they meet that deadline and provide a smooth shopping experience. Following through on commitments demonstrates professionalism and reliability, which helps build customer trust.

After a sale has been made, it is important for the seller to provide proper follow-up to the customer. This involves reaching out to make sure the product or service is working properly, resolving any issues or concerns that may arise, and making sure the customer is happy with their purchase. An effective follow-up shows the customer that the seller cares about their satisfaction and is willing to help them at any time.

The salesperson should be available to answer questions, provide additional information, and maintain open communication with the customer. This involves being attentive to customer inquiries, responding in a timely manner, and providing clear and honest answers. In addition, the seller must be transparent in their communications, avoiding exaggerations or false promises. Open and transparent communication builds trust by showing that the seller is willing to be honest and provide the necessary information.

In case problems or difficulties arise, the seller must take the initiative to solve them quickly and effectively. This involves listening to the customer's concerns, investigating the problem, and providing appropriate solutions. A successful salesperson doesn't avoid problems, but instead tackles them head-on and strives to find the best possible solution. By solving problems effectively, the customer's trust in the seller and in the brand is reinforced.

Inconsistency in treatment and service can quickly erode customer trust. Therefore, it is important for the seller to be consistent in the way they interact with customers and in the quality of service they offer. This means treating all customers, regardless of size or importance, in a courteous and professional manner, and ensuring that everyone receives the same level of high-quality care and service. Consistency in treatment and service builds trust by demonstrating that the seller is trustworthy and that a consistent level of care and satisfaction can be expected.

The development of the relationship with the client requires concrete actions on the part of the seller to strengthen trust. Fulfill agreed commitments, provide effective follow-up, maintain a lasting and prosperous relationship.

C. Maintenance of trust in the long term:

Maintaining long-term trust is essential to building strong business relationships. Let's look at some key examples of how a seller can apply these principles:

a) **Consistent Honesty and Ethics** : A successful salesperson is committed to being honest and ethical in all their interactions with customers. For example, if a customer asks about the limitations or possible challenges of a product or service, the salesperson will not hide that information. Instead, it will transparently share both the benefits and potential limitations, helping the customer make an informed decision. This consistent honesty and ethics reinforces the customer's trust in the seller and the brand.

b) **Active listening and adapting solutions:** A successful salesperson understands the importance of actively listening to the customer's needs and concerns. This involves paying attention to detail, reading between the lines, and understanding the customer's underlying motivations. For example, if a customer raises concerns about the security of a product, the vendor will not only offer standard security features, but also seek additional solutions to address the customer's specific concerns. This adaptation of solutions shows the customer that their well-being is a priority and strengthens trust in the seller.

c) **Exceptional Service and Effective Problem Solving:** A successful salesperson strives to provide exceptional service even after the sale has been made. This involves being available to the customer, responding in a timely manner to their inquiries, and resolving any issues that may arise. For example, if a customer finds a product fault after purchase, the seller will commit to resolving the problem quickly and efficiently, either by replacing the product or providing technical support. This attitude of reliability and problem solving reinforces customer confidence and demonstrates the seller's commitment to your continued satisfaction.

d) **Recognition and rectification of errors** : A successful salesperson understands that errors can occur in any business relationship. What makes the difference is how those errors are handled. If a seller makes a mistake, such as a late delivery or a misunderstanding in communication, it is important to honestly admit it and find an appropriate solution. For example, if a seller ships the wrong product, they will apologize to the customer, offer a quick solution, and compensate for any inconvenience caused. This acknowledgment and rectification approach demonstrates the integrity of the seller and helps maintain customer trust even in difficult situations.

These examples illustrate how a salesperson can maintain and nurture trust over time. By being honest, adapting solutions, providing exceptional service, and handling errors effectively, the seller lays a solid foundation for a long-lasting and successful business relationship built on mutual trust.

In summary, the three stages of building trust include first contact, relationship development, and long-term trust maintenance. By being honest, keeping promises, and providing excellent service at each of these stages, the seller can establish a strong foundation of trust with their customers, resulting in long-lasting and successful business relationships.

3. Adaptation to different communication styles:

Techniques will be explored to identify and adapt to the different communication styles of customers, thus improving the quality of interactions.

The successful salesperson understands that each customer has their own communication style, and adapting to these styles is critical to establishing an effective connection and improving the quality of interactions. Let's look at some techniques for identifying and adapting to your customers' different communication styles.

During the interaction with the customer, it is important to pay attention to both the words you use and your body language and tone of voice. By observing these signals, the closer can identify if the customer is direct and concise in their communication, or if they prefer to be more detailed and descriptive. These initial observations can help the closer tailor his own communication style to better fit the customer's. Active listening plays a crucial role in identifying different communication styles. By paying attention to how the customer formulates his ideas and how he structures his sentences, the closer can pick up on whether the customer is more analytical and logical, or whether he relies on emotions and personal experiences to express himself. By understanding the customer approach, the salesperson can tailor their own communication approach to be more effective and relevant to the customer.

To make sure they correctly understand the customer's communication style, the salesperson can ask questions and ask for clarification when necessary. This shows the customer that the closer is interested in fully understanding them and is willing to accommodate their communication style. In addition, asking pertinent questions helps deepen the understanding of the customer's needs and wants, which in turn improves the quality of the interaction. Once the closer has identified the customer's communication style, they can adjust their own language and communication structure accordingly. For example, if the customer is more detail-oriented, the salesperson may provide more specific and technically accurate information. If the customer prefers a more emotional approach, the closer can use stories or examples that appeal to the customer's emotions. Adapting the language and structure of communication helps to establish a stronger connection and facilitates mutual understanding.

By applying these techniques, the closer can improve the quality of interactions by adapting to different customer communication styles. By understanding and responding to each customer's unique communication needs, the salesperson can build a stronger and more effective relationship, which in turn contributes to sales success and customer satisfaction.

4. Demonstration of empathy:

A salesperson can demonstrate empathy by putting themselves in the customer's shoes and understanding their needs, wants, and concerns. Empathy involves showing genuine interest in the client, actively listening, showing understanding, and responding sensitively to their emotions and circumstances.

Building strong relationships is based on empathy, which allows for a deeper and more authentic connection with customers. By showing understanding and concern for their needs, customers feel valued and understood, which strengthens the business relationship and builds trust. Being an empath involves putting yourself in the client's shoes and understanding their points of view and circumstances. This helps the salesperson gain a fuller understanding of the customer's needs and desires, which in turn allows for more personalized and satisfying solutions.

Empathy allows the salesperson to understand the customer's concerns and frustrations, making it easier to identify effective solutions. By sensitively addressing customer concerns and finding solutions that fit their individual circumstances, the seller can provide quality service and lead to greater customer satisfaction.

Being empathic can be an important differentiator in a competitive market. Customers often remember and appreciate salespeople who have shown genuine care for them. This can lead to positive referrals, repeat business, and a sustainable competitive advantage. To focus on the importance of empathizing with customers, the closer must constantly remind himself that his primary goal is to satisfy customer needs and provide a positive experience. By consistently practicing empathy, the salesperson can develop strong, lasting relationships with customers, generating benefits both individually and for the company as a whole.

On the other hand, actions that would not be considered manifestations of empathy in sales are those that lack sensitivity towards the customer. For example, when a salesperson shows indifference to a customer's concerns or needs, this can create a feeling of lack of attention and consideration. Pressuring the customer to make a purchase without considering their objections or concerns is also a sign of a lack of empathy, as the customer's perspective and concerns are not being considered.

Additionally, ignoring a client's emotions or frustrations and minimizing their importance can leave the client feeling misunderstood and diminished. Empathy involves acknowledging and validating the client's emotions, providing support and understanding. It's also important to avoid a "one-size-fits-all" approach to sales, as each customer is unique and has individual needs. An empathetic salesperson adapts to the needs and preferences of each client, offering personalized solutions that fit their specific requirements.

In short, empathy in sales involves actively listening, understanding, and attending to customers' concerns, needs, and emotions. Empathetic salespeople build strong connections by demonstrating sensitivity to the customer, adapting to their individual needs, and providing personalized service. Avoiding insensitive actions, putting pressure on the customer, minimizing emotions or applying a generalized approach are key aspects of demonstrating empathy in the sales process and building lasting business relationships.

5. Keep in touch:

Staying in touch is a critical part of your sales strategy. Recognizes the importance of maintaining ongoing and consistent communication with customers, even after the initial sale has been made. This communication allows you to strengthen the customer relationship, build trust and foster long-term loyalty.

From a salesperson's point of view, in-person follow-up visits are a key strategy for maintaining a strong and satisfying relationship with customers. After closing a sale, the salesperson schedules follow-up visits to ensure customer satisfaction with the product or service purchased.

During these visits, the salesperson makes sure to address any questions or concerns the customer may have and provides additional information about new products or relevant promotions.

For example, after selling a software system to a company, the salesperson schedules a follow-up visit to make sure the customer is using the software effectively and is satisfied with the results. During the visit, the salesperson engages in an open conversation with the customer, listening to their comments and answering their questions. The vendor also takes the opportunity to introduce updates or additional features to the software that could benefit the customer. By doing so, the closer reinforces the benefits and value of their offering, while also showing a personal commitment to customer satisfaction and success.

Another example might be a gym equipment vendor who makes follow-up visits to customers after the equipment is installed. During these visits, the salesperson verifies that the equipment is working properly and meets with the customer to discuss their usage experience and any issues or concerns they may have. The salesperson also takes the opportunity to provide advice on how to maximize the benefits of the equipment and offers information on new accessories or training programs that might be of interest to the customer. These in-person visits allow the seller to establish a closer relationship with the customer and ensure continued satisfaction.

Follow-up visits in person are a valuable strategy to strengthen the relationship with clients. These visits provide an opportunity to address concerns, provide additional information, and reinforce the benefits of the seller's offer. By establishing a personal connection and demonstrating a genuine commitment to customer satisfaction, the closer can cultivate lasting relationships and build customer trust.

In addition, he uses the telephone as an effective tool to keep in touch with his customers. You make regular calls to check on their satisfaction, let them know about updates or improvements to your products and services, and offer additional support should they need it. These phone calls allow you to have more direct and personalized communication, and give you the opportunity to respond to any concerns or questions immediately.

He also takes advantage of in-person visits to establish a closer bond with his customers. During these interactions, pay close attention to their body language, facial expressions, and tone of voice to read between the lines and capture any unspoken concerns or needs. This allows you to tailor your solutions and recommendations in a personalized way, showing empathy and proving that you deeply understand your customers' needs.

Contact maintenance is considered an essential part of your sales strategy. Through in-person follow-up visits, phone calls, and the ability to read between the lines during interactions, you can communicate effectively with your customers, provide support as needed, and tailor your solutions to their individual needs. These actions allow you to establish strong and lasting business relationships, and generate a competitive advantage in the market.

6. Management of complaints and problems:

You will be taught how to effectively handle customer complaints and problems, turning them into opportunities to strengthen the relationship and improve customer satisfaction.

Complaint and problem management is an essential skill for a successful salesperson. Instead of seeing complaints and problems as obstacles, they are seen as opportunities to strengthen customer relationships and improve customer satisfaction. During the complaint and problem management process, customer concerns are addressed effectively and appropriate solutions are sought to resolve the situation.

Instead of reacting defensively or ignoring complaints, the salesperson is proactive and commits to solving the problem quickly and efficiently. You take the time to understand the situation from the customer's perspective, and you are given a safe space to vent your frustrations and expectations.

An example of complaint and problem management is when a customer complains about a faulty product they have purchased. The salesperson shows understanding of the customer's frustration and is committed to resolving the issue in a timely manner. The seller apologizes for the inconvenience caused and promises to replace the defective product immediately. In addition, the seller takes the opportunity to review internal processes and improve product quality, ensuring that similar situations do not occur again in the future.

Another example could be when a customer has a problem with the after-sales service received. The salesperson listens carefully to the customer's concerns and takes steps to investigate and resolve the problem. Open and constant communication is maintained with the client to keep them informed about the progress of the solution. In addition, the seller agrees to implement corrective measures and improvements in the after-sales service process to avoid future similar problems.

The management of complaints and problems is an opportunity to strengthen the relationship with the client and improve their satisfaction. By effectively addressing complaints and issues, the vendor demonstrates its commitment to resolving these and continually improving the quality of the product or service. The proper management of complaints and problems helps to maintain customer trust and build a lasting relationship based on satisfaction and the effective resolution of their needs.

A successful salesperson understands the importance of minimizing complaints and problems that may arise during the sales process. To achieve this, a number of proactive strategies can be applied.

First of all, it is essential to offer high-quality products or services. This means working with trusted suppliers and carrying out tests and quality checks to ensure that customers are satisfied with what they purchase. A focus on quality from the start reduces the likelihood that customers will encounter problems.

In addition, the seller must focus on clear and precise communication. It is essential to provide complete and accurate information about products or services, including features, benefits, limitations, and warranty policies. Transparent communication prevents misunderstandings and unrealistic expectations, which contributes to customer satisfaction and minimizes the possibility of complaints.

A key aspect is to identify and address objections early. During the sales process, the salesperson must be attentive to any objections or concerns that the customer may have. Rather than dismiss these concerns, the seller should proactively address them and provide additional information or clarification as needed. This helps allay customer concerns and prevents them from becoming problems later.

It is important to set realistic expectations about what the product or service can offer. Avoiding exaggerated or misleading promises is essential to avoid long-term customer dissatisfaction. By setting realistic expectations, you build a relationship based on trust and minimize the possibility of complaints.

Proper after-sales follow-up is also essential to minimize complaints and problems. After a sale has been made, the seller must maintain contact with the customer to ensure that they are satisfied with their purchase. This provides an opportunity to address any issues or concerns that may arise and take steps to resolve them in a timely manner. By showing care and concern for customer satisfaction, the relationship is strengthened and complaints are avoided.

You should look for training and professional development opportunities to improve your skills in problem solving and handling difficult situations. Learning effective communication, conflict management, and problem-solving techniques can help the salesperson better anticipate and deal with problems that may arise during the sales process.

Minimizing complaints and problems requires a proactive approach and constant attention to customer needs and concerns. By offering quality products, communicating clearly, addressing objections early, setting realistic expectations, following up properly after sales, and seeking professional development, the salesperson can maintain high customer satisfaction and minimize issues that may arise.

Companies like Amazon have managed to minimize problems and complaints through the implementation of effective customer service strategies and a focus on customer satisfaction.

Amazon has been known for its high-quality customer support. They have invested in building knowledgeable and friendly customer service teams, who are available to answer questions, resolve issues and provide support at all times. Their focus on customer satisfaction is reflected in their customer service motto: "Customer Obsessed." It has established a very favorable return and refund policy for customers. This gives them peace of mind when making purchases, knowing that they have the option to return a product if they are not satisfied or if there is a problem. This flexible policy has helped reduce complaints and has given customers confidence when shopping on Amazon.

Amazon has shown its ability to adapt and improve based on customer feedback. They have made changes to their website, shipping processes, and shopping experience in response to customer needs and expectations. This willingness to listen and act on customer feedback has been key to minimizing problems and complaints. It has used advanced technology to improve the customer experience and reduce problems. They have implemented real-time order tracking systems, personalized recommendations, and virtual assistants like Alexa to help customers with their purchases. These technological innovations have streamlined the purchasing process and reduced the chances of errors or problems.

Using Amazon's example, a seller can minimize problems and complaints by prioritizing customer satisfaction as a top priority. This means putting the customer at the center of attention and constantly looking for ways to improve their shopping experience. By offering excellent customer service, the vendor can ensure that customers' needs and concerns are addressed in an effective and timely manner. Additionally, implementing flexible return and refund policies gives customers peace of mind, allowing them to resolve any issues or dissatisfaction quickly and easily.

Also, the seller can take advantage of customer comments and reviews as a valuable source of feedback. By listening carefully to customers and using their feedback to continually improve, the salesperson demonstrates their commitment to excellence and customer satisfaction.

Technology can also be a powerful tool for improving the customer experience. By leveraging the right technology, such as customer management systems, chatbots , or communication platforms, the seller can provide quick and effective responses to customer inquiries, making it easier to resolve issues and minimizing complaints.

By applying these strategies, the seller can cultivate a strong reputation and build loyalty and trust with their customers. Like Amazon, the seller will earn their customers' trust by providing excellent service, adapting to their needs, being receptive to their feedback, and using technology effectively. This reputation for reliability and customer satisfaction will be key to minimizing problems and complaints and building long-term business relationships.

7. Generation of repeat sales:

Generating repeat sales is of great importance to a salesperson for several reasons. First, selling to existing customers is more profitable than acquiring new customers. By leveraging strong relationships already established, you can maximize customer lifetime value and grow revenue more efficiently.

Additionally, generating repeat sales involves maintaining and strengthening relationships with existing customers. This helps build trust, loyalty, and satisfaction, which in turn creates a solid foundation for future transactions and collaborations. By maintaining close communication and understanding changing customer needs, you can tailor your product or service offering to meet those specific needs, increasing the likelihood of repeat sales.

Another benefit of generating repeat sales is the power of recommendations and referrals. Satisfied and loyal customers are more likely to recommend their positive experience to others, which can lead to new business opportunities. These recommendations act as a free and trusted form of advertising, making it easier to acquire new customers.

In addition, by maintaining a long-term relationship with customers, you gain greater insight into their needs, preferences, and buying behaviors.

This allows you to tailor offers and personalize the customer experience, which in turn increases the chances of successful repeat sales.

Generating repeat sales is a key strategy for sellers as it allows them to leverage existing strong relationships, maximize revenue, build customer loyalty, and gain valuable referrals. By focusing on maintaining and cultivating these long-term relationships, sellers can build a strong and sustainable business.

An important aspect to keep in mind is to maintain regular contact with your customers to maintain an active relationship and remind them of your presence. The seller of providing exceptional service in every interaction with your customers to build trust and satisfaction. It's important to personalize offers: Use the information you have about your customers to tailor your offers and recommendations to their individual needs and preferences.

You must keep your customers informed about new products, services or improvements that may be of interest to them. By tracking past purchases, you should use tracking systems to remember your customers' past purchases and offer relevant add-on products or upgrades. Ensuring that your customers are satisfied with their purchases by offering post sales support and fixing any issues they may have.

One tactic that generates repeat sales is to organize exclusive events, invite your customers to special events, such as product launches or appreciation dinners, to strengthen the relationship and generate additional sales opportunities. Sharing relevant and useful content, such as tips, guides, or informative articles, help your customers get more out of your products or services.

Keep the delivery promise is another key point. When you always meet your commitments and delivery deadlines, you will generate trust and security in your customers.

The successful salesperson recognizes and celebrates special occasions for their customers, such as their birthday or business anniversary, to maintain an emotional bond and generate new sales leads.

Remember that these tactics should be tailored to your industry and type of business, but in general, they are focused on maintaining an active and personalized relationship with your customers, providing excellent service, and finding ways to continually add value.

The Mattress Saleswoman

Sandra, an experienced mattress salesperson, was known for her ability to build lasting and meaningful relationships with her clients. A notable example of her success in this regard was her relationship with a client named Carlos.

Carlos was a recurring client of Sandra's. I had purchased several mattresses from her over the years and was always pleased with the quality and service I received. However, on one occasion, Carlos found himself in a challenging situation. He had been in an accident that left him with a medical condition that required a specialized mattress to improve his comfort and recovery.

Sandra, aware of Carlos' situation and his loyalty as a client, decided to take a personalized approach to help him. Rather than simply offer him a standard mattress, he decided to research and learn more about the options available to meet Carlos's specific needs.

After consulting with experts and providers, Sandra found a specialized mattress that was designed to provide the support and comfort needed for Carlos' medical condition. She met with him and explained the features and benefits of the mattress in detail, making sure Carlos understood how it could help him in his recovery process.

However, the specialized mattress had a higher price compared to conventional mattresses. Carlos expressed concern about the cost and his financial limitations.

Sandra recognized Carlos' concern and worked collaboratively with him to find a solution. They negotiated an installment payment plan that suited Carlos's financial possibilities, allowing him to purchase the mattress without creating an undue financial burden.

Throughout the process, Sandra maintained constant communication with Carlos. Provided updates on the progress of your order, answered your questions, and provided additional mattress care and maintenance tips.

The relationship between Sandra and Carlos grew even stronger as they worked together to overcome challenges and meet Carlos' specific needs. Sandra not only sold a mattress, but also became a trusted advisor to Carlos, providing him with personalized service and solutions tailored to his situation.

In the following years, Sandra continued to provide support and follow-up to Carlos. He kept abreast of her health condition and offered extra assistance when needed. In addition, Sandra took the opportunity to introduce Carlos to new products and accessories related to mattress care and improving his quality of life.

The relationship between Sandra and Carlos demonstrated that a salesperson focused on building lasting relationships can turn a specific need into an opportunity to provide exceptional and personalized service. Through her dedication, empathy and continuous attention, Sandra achieved not only Carlos' satisfaction, but also his loyalty and trust as a long-term client.

Chapter 4:
Overcoming Objections and Handling Rejections

Objections are the concerns, doubts or resistance that customers raise during the sales process. These objections can arise due to various reasons, such as lack of information, price, competition, uncertainty or unmet needs. Objections are a natural part of the sales process and can be viewed as barriers that must be overcome to make the sale.

The lack of information from the client can represent a challenge in the sales process. When a customer does not have access to enough information about a product or service, doubts and concerns naturally arise. Uncertainty can generate resistance to making the purchase, since the customer does not feel sure of the benefits that can be obtained or if the product or service will satisfy their needs.

Today, we live in an information-saturated digital environment, where consumers are constantly exposed to a plethora of advertisements, promotional messages, and online content. This information overload can be overwhelming for many customers and make it difficult for them to find relevant and accurate information about a particular product or service.

The proliferation of communication channels, such as social media, websites, and emails, has expanded the amount of information consumers are exposed to on a daily basis. Every time they browse the Internet, check their social networks or open their email inbox, they are faced with numerous advertising and promotional messages trying to grab their attention.

This constant flood of information can lead to a feeling of confusion and difficulty distinguishing between what is relevant and what is not. Customers may feel overwhelmed by the number of options available and may have difficulty finding the accurate and reliable information they are looking for.

The brevity of online advertising and promotional messages may limit the amount of detail and context that can be provided. In a limited space, it is difficult to convey all the information necessary for customers to make an informed decision about a product or service.

As a result, some customers may find themselves disoriented and confused about the features, benefits, and value of a particular product or service. This lack of information can lead to doubts and resistance to making a purchase, as customers may feel insecure or distrustful due to a lack of clarity and understanding.

The Internet and social networks have democratized the generation and dissemination of information. Anyone can create and share content online, which means there is a wide range of sources and opinions available. However, this democratization can also lead to the proliferation of false, inaccurate or biased information.

By establishing a trusting relationship with the customer, the salesperson can position themselves as a trusted and accessible resource to answer any additional questions and provide personalized guidance. This involves actively listening to the client's needs and concerns and tailoring the information provided to address their specific concerns.

Information overload in the digital age can make it difficult for customers to find relevant and accurate information about a product or service. As a salesperson, it is important to recognize this situation and provide clear, concise, and personalized communication that highlights the benefits and value of the product or service, establishing a trusting relationship, and offering additional guidance based on individual customer needs.

Not all available information is reliable or accurate. Customers face the challenge of filtering and discerning between useful and unhelpful information. This difficulty in filtering information can lead to a lack of confidence in the validity and accuracy of what they find, which in turn can result in a lack of solid knowledge about a particular product or service.

For clients, it can be challenging to identify which information is trustworthy and which is not. They may come across conflicting opinions, unverified data, or even misleading information. This can lead to doubts and skepticism regarding the information they find, especially when it comes to products or services that are important or expensive.

As a marketer, it's essential to recognize this information overload and address it proactively. It is important to offer clear and concise communication that highlights the most relevant and valuable aspects of the product or service. Providing practical examples, testimonials from satisfied customers, and clear explanations of how the product or service addresses the customer's needs and wants can help overcome confusion and provide the information needed to make an informed decision. It is critical to recognize this difficulty and address it proactively. It is important to provide information that is reliable, verifiable, and supported by evidence. This may include citing reputable sources, sharing relevant studies or research, and providing testimonials from satisfied customers.

Another reason for objections may be lack of time, which is a reality for many clients in today's society. Although information is widely available, people may be busy with various responsibilities and commitments that limit their ability to fully investigate a product or service. This can make it difficult for them to access complete and detailed information about what they are considering buying.

Let's imagine a client who works long hours and has a family to care for. Your free time is limited and you must prioritize your activities. When you find yourself in need of purchasing a product or contracting a service, you may not have the time to fully investigate all the available options. As a result, you may make decisions based on cursory information or quick recommendations without fully analyzing the features, pros, and cons of each option.

Another practical example is a client who is planning a vacation and looking for a hotel. However, your time is busy with work and other personal matters, making it difficult for you to spend hours researching different hotels, reading reviews, comparing prices, and looking for recommendations. Instead, you may make a quick decision based on the limited information you find in banner ads or the first few options that appear in search results.

In both cases, the lack of time limits the client's ability to obtain a complete and detailed vision of the available options. This can result in hasty or incomplete decisions, which in turn can increase the likelihood of dissatisfaction or regret later.

As a salesperson, it is important to take into account this lack of time and adapt to the needs of the client. Various strategies can be implemented to make it easier for them to obtain relevant information and make informed decisions, such as:

a. **Synthesize the key information** : Present in a clear and concise way the most relevant points about the product or service, highlighting its main benefits and how it can satisfy the customer's needs. Provide information that is easily digestible and understandable in a short period of time.

b. **Offer head-to-head comparisons:** Present clear comparisons between different options or competitors, highlighting key differences in terms of features, pricing, and benefits. This allows the client to make faster and more efficient decisions by having a clear vision of the available options.

c. **Provide trusted testimonials and reviews:** Include testimonials from satisfied customers and verified reviews to help the customer gain perspective from others who have already experienced the product or service. This allows you to gain a quick insight into the experiences of others and reduce the time it takes to search for additional information.

d. **Offer Personalized Advice:** Be proactive in providing recommendations based on customer needs and preferences. Listen carefully to their requirements and offer solutions that fit their particular circumstances, saving them time searching for options themselves.

Lack of time can make it difficult for customers to spend enough time to thoroughly research a product or service. As a seller, strategies can be implemented to make it easier for them to obtain information

Price and competition are common factors that can generate objections from customers during the sales process. These elements can influence the perception of value and purchase decision-making.

Price is one of the most obvious factors that can raise objections. Customers may consider that the price of a product or service is too high in relation to their perception of its value or in comparison with other alternatives available on the market. They may object that the price is inaccessible to their budget or that they are not willing to pay that amount for the product or service in question.

On the other hand, the existence of competitors in the market can generate objections from customers. They may object that there are cheaper or higher quality alternatives on the market offered by direct competitors. If customers perceive that there are more attractive or competitive options, they may be reluctant to purchase the product or service offered by the seller.

Facing objections related to price and competition requires specific skills and strategies on the part of the seller. Some techniques to overcome these objections could be:

a) *Highlight the value*: Explain and clearly demonstrate the added value offered by the product or service in relation to its price. Highlight the benefits and unique features that set you apart from the competition, and how they justify the price.

b) *Cost and benefit comparisons:* Compare the price of the product or service with the benefits and advantages it provides in the long term. Show how the initial investment translates into saving time, efficiency, quality or long-term satisfaction.

c) *Offer options and customization:* Provide different pricing options or packages that suit the customer's needs and budget.

This allows the client to find an option that adjusts to their economic capacity and that still meets their requirements.

d) **Highlight Competitive Advantages:** Highlight the unique features and advantages of the product or service compared to direct competitors. Show how it differs and why it is worth paying a slightly higher price for that difference.

e) **Offer guarantees and return policies** : Provide satisfaction guarantees, refunds or flexible return policies. This provides peace of mind for the customer as they know they have the ability to change their mind or receive a refund if they are not satisfied with their purchase.

It is important to remember that each client is unique and may have different objections. The successful salesperson must listen carefully to the customer's concerns, understand their needs, and tailor their response strategies based on each particular situation.

Uncertainty and unmet needs are two common factors that can lead to customer objections. When a customer feels uncertain or has unmet needs, they are more likely to express objections or doubts before making a purchase decision.

Uncertainty can arise when the customer does not have enough information about the product or service they are considering. You may have questions about its operation, features, or specific benefits. In addition, the lack of trust in the brand or in the reputation of the seller can also generate uncertainty in the client. For example, in the telecommunications segment, a customer may have objections due to a lack of clarity about network coverage, quality of service, or associated additional costs.

Unmet needs can also raise objections. If the customer feels that their needs are not being addressed or that the product or service does not meet their expectations, they are likely to express objections. For example, in the field of telecommunications, a customer may have a need for a higher internet speed or a better quality of the telephone signal. If a well-known brand in this sector does not meet these needs effectively, the customer is likely to raise objections and look for alternatives.

In the case of AT&T, a well-known telecommunications brand, uncertainty may have arisen in relation to aspects such as network coverage, service quality or associated costs. However, AT&T was able to provide clear and transparent network coverage information, highlighting the breadth and reliability of its network in different locations. In addition, they made investments in infrastructure and technology to improve the quality of service and provide a smooth and reliable experience for customers. In terms of costs, AT&T was able to offer flexible plan and promotion options that fit customers' needs and budgets, providing price transparency and avoiding hidden costs.

By addressing these objections, AT&T was able to build trust with its customers and demonstrate its commitment to customer satisfaction. By providing solutions to customers' needs and concerns, AT&T was able to strengthen its market position and generate repeat sales. Their focus on improving the customer experience and providing quality service allowed them to overcome initial objections and build strong relationships with their customers.

Accurate communication and effective salesperson interaction are key elements in turning objections into opportunities. Through clear and transparent communication, the seller can address objections related to lack of information, providing relevant details and answering customer questions accurately and completely.

The seller must highlight the value and benefits of the product or service, showing how its price is justified in relation to the quality and results it offers. In addition, you can offer flexible pricing and promotion options to suit the customer's needs and budget.

Regarding the competition, the seller must highlight the key advantages and differences of his product or service compared to competitors, showing how he can best meet the needs of the customer. You can provide factual comparisons and concrete evidence to support your argument.

To address uncertainty, the seller may offer guarantees, testimonials from satisfied customers, and examples of success stories. You may also provide additional information, such as technical specifications, tests, or certifications, to support the reliability and quality of the product or service.

When dealing with unmet needs, the salesperson must use active listening to understand the customer's needs and adapt their approach accordingly. You can offer customized solutions and highlight how your product or service can effectively meet those specific needs.

Through accurate communication and effective interaction, the salesperson can turn objections into opportunities by providing accurate information, highlighting value and benefits, overcoming competitor concerns, addressing uncertainty, and offering solutions tailored to customer needs. . This builds trust, establishes a strong relationship, and increases the chances of closing the sale.

The rejection of sales is defined as the refusal or resistance by the customer to purchase a product or service offered by the seller. It is important to note that rejection is a natural part of the sales process and can have a variety of causes.

A real example of refusal to sell can be when a customer visits an electronics store and the seller presents a state-of-the-art television with all its features and benefits. However, the customer is hesitant and ultimately decides not to make the purchase. In this case, the rejection can be due to different reasons, such as the customer does not consider the necessary product at that moment, the price is higher than expected, or the customer has a preference for another brand or model.

Another example can be when a salesperson tries to sell a consulting service to a company, but the client states that they already have a similar service provider and are satisfied with their performance. In this case, the rejection is due to the fact that the customer does not see the need to change providers or considers that their current provider meets their expectations. Rejection may be the result of unresolved objections, lack of interest, incompatibility with customer needs, or external factors.

Handling rejection is a fundamental skill for a successful salesperson. Here are five steps a salesperson can take to handle rejection effectively:

The first step in handling sales rejection is not to take it personally. It is essential to understand that the rejection is not directed at you as a person, but at the product or service offer that you are presenting. By keeping this perspective, you prevent rejection from emotionally affecting you and undermining your confidence in yourself as a salesperson.

When you get a "no" for an answer, it's important not to get carried away by frustration or demotivation. Instead, you should maintain a positive and professional attitude. Recognize that rejection is an inevitable part of the sales process and that every "no" brings you closer to a "yes." Keep your focus on long-term goals and don't let individual rejection affect your overall performance.

An effective way to not take it personally is to separate your personal identity from your role as a salesperson. Remember that you are offering a product or service and that rejection does not imply a judgment about your worth as a person. Also, keep in mind that each customer has their own unique needs, circumstances, and preferences, and rejection may simply reflect a misalignment between what you offer and what the customer is currently looking for.

By maintaining a positive and professional attitude, you will be able to handle rejection more effectively and move forward with confidence. Use rejection as an opportunity to learn and improve your sales skills, and remember that every interaction is a new opportunity to succeed.

The second crucial step in handling rejection effectively is listening to and understanding the customer's concerns and objections. This involves paying active attention to what the client is expressing, both verbally and non-verbally. By listening carefully, you will be able to pick up on the customer's underlying concerns and understand the reasons behind their rejection.

It is important to show empathy towards the client and try to put yourself in their place. This involves understanding their perspective, needs and expectations. By doing so, you will be better equipped to address their concerns effectively and offer relevant solutions.

During this process, it's important to avoid interrupting the client or automatically advocating your position. Instead, ask open-ended questions to get more information and deepen their point of view. This will help you demonstrate genuine interest in their concerns and build a stronger connection with the customer.

Plus, by understanding customer concerns and objections, you'll be able to fine-tune your sales approach and customize your offer to address their specific needs. This will increase the likelihood of overcoming objections and reaching a mutually beneficial agreement.
By listening carefully and understanding customer concerns and objections, you will be in a strong position to effectively address their concerns and offer solutions that meet their needs. This will strengthen the relationship with the client and increase the chances of closing a successful sale.

The third step is to be empathetic. When a client expresses some concerns and objections, it is important to respond with empathy. This involves showing understanding of their views and showing that you care about their perspective. You can use phrases like "I understand your concerns" or "I can see why you're worried about that" to validate their feelings.

Once you've shown empathy, it's time to look for solutions that can meet the customer's needs. This involves listening carefully to your concerns and working together to find viable alternatives. You can present different options or approaches that address their concerns and resolve the issues they are experiencing.

It is important to adapt your approach during this stage and to be flexible in finding solutions. You can ask additional questions to better understand the customer's specific needs and offer additional benefits that can help overcome their objections. For example, you can highlight unique features of your product or service that directly address their concerns and offer special discounts to encourage their decision.

The key is to offer personalized solutions and show the client that you care about their satisfaction. By doing so, you are building a trusting relationship and showing your commitment to providing them with a positive experience. Remember that every objection is an opportunity to find a solution that benefits both the customer and you as a seller.

Responding with empathy and solutions involves showing understanding of the customer's concerns and actively seeking ways to meet their needs. By presenting alternatives, adapting your approach, and offering additional benefits, you can overcome their objections and strengthen the customer relationship.

The fourth step, "Reinforce Value," is crucial in handling rejection and turning it into a sales opportunity. Here it is about clearly and persuasively communicating the value and benefits of the product or service you are offering. The main idea is to highlight how your offer can solve specific problems or satisfy customer needs in a way that is superior to the competition.

To reinforce value, it is important to use effective communication techniques. Some strategies you can employ include:

a. **Identify the key points:** Determine the most relevant and attractive aspects of your product or service that are relevant to the customer's needs and concerns. These points may include special features, unique functionality, proven results, testimonials from satisfied customers, awards or recognition earned, among others.

b. **Personalization** : Adapt your message and examples to the specific situation and needs of the client. Show how your offer is a perfect fit for their circumstances and how it can make a real difference in their life or business.

c. **Hands-on demos** : If possible, offer hands-on demos or concrete examples to illustrate how your product or service addresses customer challenges. This can help visualize value and benefits in action.

d. **Competitive Comparison** : Highlight competitive advantages and key differences between your offering and those of your competition.

You can highlight aspects such as superior quality, more competitive price, specialized technical support, faster delivery times, etc.

e.   **Respond to objections** : Anticipate and address possible objections that the client may have. Prepare clear and convincing responses to counter any doubts or concerns. This demonstrates your knowledge of the product and your willingness to resolve any issues that may arise.

Remember that reinforcing value is not just about talking about product features, but about showing how those features translate into tangible benefits and solutions to specific customer problems. By clearly communicating the value and benefits of your offer, you can influence customer decision-making and overcome any objections that may have been raised initially.

The fifth step, **"Move Forward"** , is critical to the success of the seller. It's important to understand that rejection is part of the sales process and not all customers will be willing to buy at any given time. Learning from experience and moving forward are key aspects of this step.

It is important to take rejection as a learning opportunity. Instead of feeling discouraged, reflect on the customer interaction and look for possible areas of improvement. Discuss how you could better address objections in the future and how to improve your overall sales approach.

Maintaining a positive mindset is essential in handling rejection. As daunting as it may be, remember that every rejection brings you closer to a successful sale. Visualize success and maintain confidence in your abilities and the value of your product or service. An optimistic attitude will help you overcome obstacles and maintain momentum.

Looking for new opportunities is another important aspect. Instead of getting caught up in individual rejection, direct your energy towards finding new opportunities. Explore different market segments, search for leads in different industries, or use different sales approaches. Expand your network of contacts and stay open to new possibilities.

Persistence and perseverance are indispensable qualities in handling rejection. Don't give in easily to rejection. Keep pushing yourself and improving your skills. Remember that every interaction is an opportunity to learn and grow as a salesperson. Maintain determination and discipline to achieve your goals.

If you find recurring patterns of rejection, consider adapting your sales approach. Analyze how you could improve your presentation, your communication strategy or even your product or service. Adjust your approach based on feedback and past experiences. The ability to adapt will help you overcome obstacles and find new ways to approach customers.

"Move Forward" step involves learning from experience, maintaining a positive mindset, seeking out new opportunities, persisting, and adapting as necessary. By doing so, a salesperson can turn rejection into an opportunity to grow, improve, and achieve sales success.
By following these steps, a salesperson can handle rejection constructively and turn it into an opportunity to learn, improve their sales approach, and strengthen their ability to close future sales.

Both situations, objections and rejection, are challenges salespeople face in their work. However, a successful salesperson knows that these situations are not necessarily final and can become opportunities to persuade the customer, demonstrate the value of the product or service, resolve concerns, and ultimately close the sale.

When great salespeople encounter objections from customers, they adopt a positive mindset and view these objections as opportunities rather than obstacles. Instead of seeing them as a barrier to closing the sale, they understand that objections are an invitation to dig deeper into the customer's needs and concerns.

To change the perspective, the seller must focus on providing more information and demonstrating the value of their product or service. They view the objection as an opportunity to educate the customer and provide additional information to help them make an informed decision. Rather than simply trying to overcome the objection, great salespeople see this as an opportunity to engage the customer in a meaningful conversation. They listen carefully to the customer's concerns and strive to understand the root of the objection.

They use this opportunity to highlight the benefits and unique features of their product or service, and how they can meet specific customer needs. They use concrete examples and success stories to support their arguments and demonstrate the real value that their offer can bring to the customer.

By shifting the perspective and seeing objections as opportunities, great salespeople can build a stronger customer relationship. The customer feels heard and valued, and appreciates the salesperson's effort to address their concerns. This can lead to greater trust and willingness on the part of the customer to consider the offer and ultimately make the purchase.

Changing perspective is a key strategy used by great salespeople to turn objections into opportunities. They see these objections as an invitation to dig deeper into the customer's needs and concerns, and they use this opportunity to provide more information, demonstrate the value of their product or service, and build a strong customer relationship.

The closer should use open questions as a powerful tool to fully understand the objection and discover the real reasons behind it. Open questions are those that cannot be answered with a simple "yes" or "no" but require a more detailed response from the customer.

By asking open-ended questions, the closer demonstrates a genuine interest in understanding the customer's concerns and needs. These questions invite the customer to share more information, providing the closer a clearer view of what is driving the objection.

Some examples of open-ended questions that salespeople can use include:

- "Could you explain more about your concern about [objection]?"
- "What is most important to you when considering [product/service]?"
- "What would you like to achieve by resolving this objection?"

- "What are your expectations in terms of [aspect related to the objection]?"

These open-ended questions not only allow the salesperson to obtain additional information about the objection, but also help establish more open and collaborative communication with the customer. As the customer shares more details, the salesperson can identify underlying concerns and discover opportunities to resolve them effectively.

Importantly, the closer should listen carefully to the customer's responses and avoid interrupting or judging. The idea is to fully understand the objection and create space for a deeper and more meaningful conversation.

By using open-ended questions effectively, salespeople can uncover the real reasons behind the objection and address them in a more precise and personalized way. This allows them to turn the objection into an opportunity to demonstrate the value of their product or service and find solutions that meet the customer's needs.

When convincing the customer directly may not be effective, the seller focuses on demonstrating the value of his offer in a tangible and convincing way. They use various strategies to support their arguments and overcome customer doubts or concerns:

a.   **Concrete Examples:** Successful salespeople use specific examples to illustrate how their product or service has helped other customers in similar situations. They can tell success stories or describe real situations where their offer has solved problems and generated positive results. These concrete examples help the customer to visualize how your product or service can benefit them.

b.   **Case studies:** Case studies are a powerful tool to demonstrate the value of an offer. The great sellers present real cases in which their product or service has generated significant improvements in the companies or has satisfied the needs of the clients. Case studies provide tangible evidence of the benefits and results that can be achieved.

c. **Testimonials from satisfied customers:** Testimonials from satisfied customers are an effective way to demonstrate the value of an offer. Great sellers collect testimonials from happy customers who have experienced the benefits of their product or service. These testimonials act as social proof and build customer trust by showing that other people have had positive experiences.

d. **Relevant data:** Data and statistics can support the seller's arguments by providing objective evidence. Great sellers use relevant and credible data to support claims about the effectiveness, quality, or performance of their offering. This data can come from market research, independent studies or internal metrics that demonstrate the results obtained by other clients.

e. **Clear benefits** : Great salespeople focus on clearly communicating the benefits that the customer will get from purchasing their product or service. They highlight how your offering can solve specific problems, improve efficiency, increase productivity, or save time and money. By clearly and concisely demonstrating the benefits, salespeople help the customer understand the value they will receive.

Demonstration of value by great sellers relies on providing concrete examples, using case studies, testimonials from satisfied customers, and relevant data. These strategies support your arguments, build customer trust, and help you overcome objections by showing how your offering can meet their needs and deliver positive results.

When it comes to turning objections into opportunities, solution customization is a key approach used by large vendors. They recognize that each customer is unique and has individual needs, so they avoid offering generic answers or standard solutions. Instead, they tailor their approach to specifically address customer concerns and offer tailored solutions to suit their circumstances and requirements.

To achieve this, great salespeople spend time actively listening to the customer. They pay attention to your concerns, questions, and specific needs. They use empathic listening skills to fully understand the customer's situation and get a clear picture of what really concerns them.

Once they've captured the customer's concerns, the large vendors work collaboratively with them to design a custom solution. This involves presenting options and recommendations that directly address the concerns raised. They can offer relevant examples or success stories that demonstrate how their product or service has solved similar problems in the past.

In addition, large vendors ensure that the custom solution is aligned with the client's goals and priorities. This involves highlighting the specific benefits and advantages that matter most to the customer, and how the proposed solution can help them achieve their goals. They are also willing to make adjustments and adaptations to the solution to meet changing customer needs.

By offering a personalized solution, you show the customer that you are paying attention to them and that their objection is being taken seriously. This builds trust and shows the customer that you are willing to go above and beyond to meet their individual needs. As a result, the customer feels valued and is more likely to view the seller's offer as a genuine solution to his problem.

Solution customization involves tailoring the approach and offering specific responses to customer concerns. Great vendors understand the importance of treating each customer as unique and strive to offer solutions that address their individual needs. In doing so, they build trust, demonstrate value, and turn objections into opportunities to close the sale.

When we see an objection that cannot be resolved directly, they use the strategy of offering alternatives to the client. This tactic allows them to show flexibility and adaptability in finding solutions that meet customer needs.

First, they suggest additional options that address the customer's specific concern. For example, if the customer finds the price too high, the seller may offer different packages or pricing plans to fit their budget. In this way, the seller demonstrates that he understands the customer's concern and seeks to find a solution that meets his needs.

In addition, complementary features can be identified that add value to the main product or service and resolve the customer objection. For example, if the customer is concerned about a product's durability, the salesperson may highlight additional strength features or extended warranties that provide additional peace of mind for the customer.

In some cases, the customer objection may be related to a specific need that the current product or service cannot meet. In this case, the big sellers can recommend complementary products or services that fill that need. For example, if the customer is looking for a comprehensive solution, the vendor may offer additional installation, maintenance, or technical support services.

Another effective strategy is to offer free demos or trials. If the customer has concerns about the functionality or effectiveness of the product, the seller can offer the opportunity to experience it for himself. This gives them the ability to overcome the objection by providing tangible evidence of product quality and performance.

Finally, in certain cases, personalized advice can be offered to help the client find the best solution for their need. This involves listening carefully to the client's concerns, understanding their situation, and recommending options that fit their specific circumstances.

Turn objections into opportunities by offering alternatives that address customer concerns and meet customer needs. These alternatives may include additional options, add-on features, add-on products or services, free demos or trials, and personalized advice. By implementing these strategies, salespeople demonstrate their commitment to finding the right solutions and establish a relationship of trust with the customer.

Handling emotional objections is a key skill in turning objections into opportunities. When a client raises an objection based on negative emotions or past experiences, it is important to approach it in an empathetic and understanding manner. First, the salesperson acknowledges the customer's emotions and validates them. They can say something like, "I understand that this situation may cause concern or frustration." By acknowledging emotions, the closer shows empathy and shows that they care about the customer's feelings.

Then, it seeks to understand the reasons behind those emotions. You can ask open-ended questions to allow the client to express their concerns and past experiences. By actively listening, the closer can better understand the customer's perspective and find common ground.

Once a mutual understanding has been established, the closer can work with the customer to overcome those emotional objections. This involves providing additional information, sharing testimonials or success stories that address those specific concerns. They may also offer alternative solutions or tailor the offer to meet the emotional needs of the customer.

Building a trusting relationship is critical in handling emotional objections. Great salespeople strive to establish and maintain that relationship through empathy and genuine care. By showing understanding and concern for the client's emotions, they can create an environment of mutual trust that makes it easier to overcome emotional objections.

Handling emotional objections involves acknowledging and validating the client's emotions, understanding their reasons, and working together to overcome those objections. Through empathy and trust-building, great salespeople can turn these emotional objections into opportunities to demonstrate value and the ability to meet customer needs.

The track and trace step is critical for big sellers. After addressing an objection and providing a satisfactory response, they don't stop there, but continue the process to ensure customer satisfaction and strengthen the relationship.

Follow-up involves contacting the customer after their objection has been addressed. It can be done through a phone call, email, or even a face-to-face meeting, depending on the client's preference. The goal is to check if the customer is satisfied with the response provided and if their concerns have been fully addressed.

During follow-up, commitment and customer service must be shown. They actively listen to any additional feedback the customer may have and are willing to take further action if necessary. This shows the customer that their satisfaction and success are a priority for the seller.

In addition, follow-up provides an opportunity to further strengthen the relationship with the customer. During these follow-up interactions, big sellers can take the opportunity to provide additional information, share relevant updates, or even offer exclusive promotions or discounts. This helps to maintain the client's interest and build a long-term relationship based on trust and satisfaction.

Follow-up and follow-up are essential in turning objections into opportunities. This step demonstrates commitment, care and concern for customer satisfaction. By following the follow-up process, great sellers can ensure that the customer is satisfied with the response, resolve any additional concerns, and strengthen the relationship for the long term.

Remember that the key to turning objections into opportunities lies in listening carefully, demonstrating value, personalizing the solution, and staying positive and proactive. Every objection is an opportunity to deepen your relationship with the customer and demonstrate the unique value of your offer.

Here is a list of things that a seller can have ready to face possible objections and rejections:

1. Knowledge of the product or service: Make sure you have in-depth and up-to-date knowledge about the product or service you are selling. This will allow you to accurately and convincingly respond to any objections related to its functionality, features, benefits, and competitive advantages.

2. Identification of common objections: Analyze the most common objections that customers usually raise and prepare to address them effectively. Identify the most frequent concerns and develop responses and strong arguments to counter them.

3. Practice responses and arguments : Spend time practicing and perfecting your responses to objections. Rehearse different scenarios and examples to make sure your arguments are clear, persuasive, and convincing.

4. Collection of testimonials and success stories : Collect testimonials from satisfied customers and success stories that support the effectiveness of your product or service. These testimonials can be used as social proof to counter objections and demonstrate the value of what you are selling.

5. Preparation of supporting materials: Prepare supporting materials, such as brochures, presentations or demonstrations, that support your arguments and help to dispel customer doubts. These materials must be clear, visually appealing, and provide relevant information about the product or service.

6. Develop Active Listening Skills: Make sure you develop active listening skills to fully understand customer objections and concerns. This will allow you to address them more effectively and tailor your responses to their specific needs.

7. Keep calm and professionalism: In the face of objections and rejections, it is essential to remain calm and professional. Avoid reacting defensively. Instead, show empathy, listen carefully, and respond in a respectful and polite manner.

8. Focus on problem solving: Instead of viewing objections as barriers, focus on finding solutions. Approaches customer concerns with a problem-solving mindset and shows willingness to find alternatives or make adjustments as needed.

9. Adaptability and flexibility: Be prepared to adapt to different scenarios and individual customer needs. Not all objections are created equal, so be willing to adjust your approach and offer custom solutions for each situation.

10. Self-confidence and positive attitude : Maintain a positive attitude and trust in your skills as a salesperson. Confidence in yourself and what you are selling will reflect in your interactions with customers and help you overcome objections and rejections effectively.

Remember that this list is a general guide and each seller can adapt it according to their needs and sales style. The important thing is to be prepared.

The Bubble Seller

Once upon a time there was a soap bubble seller who walked the streets of a picturesque town. He had with him a small cart full of containers of soap solution and magic wands to create bubbles. His goal was to bring joy and fun to people, especially children.

As he walked through the streets, the bubble seller was met with various objections. Some said that soap bubbles were brittle and would burst easily. Others considered that it was an ephemeral product and not worth investing in.

However, the bubble seller was not deterred by these objections. Instead of seeing them as obstacles, he saw them as opportunities to demonstrate the value of his product. Every time someone raised an objection, the bubble seller would smile and ask them to wait a moment.

Then, with his magic wand, the salesman would create a huge soap bubble. He would lift it up in the air and blow it gently, showing everyone the beauty and delicacy of the bubble. People were amazed to see how it floated in the wind, reflecting the colors of the rainbow and filling the air with its iridescent brilliance. The bubble seller explained that while bubbles may appear fragile, they are also symbols of joy and fleeting moments of fun.

Then, with a smile, the bubble seller would challenge those who were in doubt to try to burst the bubble. He would hand them a wand and encourage them to blow gently on the bubble. To everyone's surprise, the bubble resisted, floating in the air without bursting.

People, amazed and excited, were beginning to realize that soap bubbles were not as fragile as they seemed. They were magical moments of happiness and entertainment, capable of capturing the imagination of children and adults alike. The bubble seller reminded them that although bubbles eventually fade, they leave an imprint of joy and lasting memories in people's hearts.

This story of the bubble seller teaches us that objections can become opportunities if we face them with creativity and perseverance. Instead of giving in to doubts and skepticism, we can show the value of our product or service in a tangible way and demonstrate how it can enrich people's lives.

Just as the bubble salesman turned objections into admiration and appreciation, we too can find ways to overcome objections and turn them into opportunities to strengthen our customer relationships and achieve sales success.

Chapter 5:
Closing of Sales and Negotiation

The four closing techniques are specific approaches salespeople use to guide the customer toward the final purchase decision and close the sale.

Option Closure : This technique involves presenting the customer with two or more options to choose from.

Closing by assumption: In this technique, the closer assumes that the customer has already made the decision to buy and proceeds to guide him to the next step.

Closing due to urgency: This technique is based on creating a sense of urgency in the client so that they make an immediate decision.

Closing by Questions: This technique involves asking the customer questions that are designed to lead him to the conclusion that the product or service satisfies his needs or wants.

Option closeout

Option closing is a sales technique that involves presenting the customer with two or more options to choose from. The idea behind this technique is to give the customer a sense of control and participation in the buying process, which can help overcome indecision and facilitate decision-making.

In practice, the seller can present the customer with different options that fit his needs and preferences. For example, in clothing sales, you can offer different styles, sizes, or colors for the customer to choose from. In the sale of electronic products, different models can be offered with different characteristics and prices.

Before presenting the options, it is important to know your client well and understand their needs and preferences. This will allow you to offer relevant and personalized options.

Knowing your customer is an essential aspect of the sales process. Before presenting options, it is essential to thoroughly understand who your customer is and what their needs and preferences are. This will allow you to offer personalized and relevant solutions that fit their specific requirements.

To achieve good customer knowledge, it is important to employ different strategies. First, do extensive research on your client and their industry. Examine their website, social media profiles, and any other relevant sources to gain insight into their goals, challenges, and market trends. This research will give you a deeper understanding of their business and help you tailor your options to their unique needs.

In addition to research, it's crucial to actively listen to your customer during interactions. Pay attention to their comments, questions, and concerns. Listen with empathy and show genuine interest in understanding their needs. This will allow you to gain valuable information and adjust your options accordingly.

To establish a strong relationship with your customers, it is essential to know them thoroughly and understand their needs and preferences. A key strategy to achieve this is to keep up-to-date records of your interactions and transactions with each customer.

Keeping accurate and up-to-date records allows you to have a complete picture of each customer's preferences, purchase history, and specific needs. This gives you an invaluable advantage in presenting customized options to suit your requirements. By keeping an organized record of past conversations, stated preferences, and any relevant details, you can show a high level of care and attention when interacting with your customers.

Up-to-date records also allow you to effectively follow up with your customers. You can follow up after each sale to make sure they are happy with their purchase and resolve any issues or concerns that may arise. You can also take advantage of logs to proactively follow up on future interactions. For example, if a customer expressed interest in a specific product in the past, you can remind them of that conversation and present additional options related to their needs and preferences.

Technology plays a crucial role in keeping records up to date. Using a customer relationship management (CRM) system or any other digital tool helps you efficiently capture and store relevant customer data. These tools allow you to record important details such as contact dates, preferences, purchase history and any other relevant information to provide personalized service and excel in your customer service.

Keeping up-to-date records is essential to building lasting relationships with your customers. By having access to accurate and up-to-date information, you can offer personalized options that meet their needs, follow up proactively, and provide exceptional service. This not only builds customer loyalty, but also strengthens your reputation as a trustworthy seller who is attentive to the needs of your customers.

Asking clear and open questions is also an effective technique to get to know your customer better. Ask strategic questions that help you understand their goals, challenges, preferences, and expectations. These questions should be broad enough to encourage a deeper conversation and reveal important information to tailor your options.

Additionally, it is critical to keep up-to-date records of your customer interactions. Keep an organized record of conversations, preferences, and specific needs. This will allow you to carry out an effective and personalized follow-up in future interactions, which demonstrates your commitment and customer service.

By knowing your customer in depth, you can offer personalized and relevant options that align with their needs. This creates an environment of trust and demonstrates your commitment to provide solutions tailored to their requirements. A personalized approach increases the chances that the customer will feel valued and engaged in the buying process, which can lead to a stronger and more lasting relationship.

While it's good to provide options, offering too many options can overwhelm the customer. It is advisable to limit the options to a manageable number to facilitate decision making.

- *Limit Options*

Offering options is an effective closing strategy, but it's important to keep in mind that offering too many options can overwhelm the customer and make it difficult for them to make decisions. This is why it is recommended to limit the options to a manageable number to facilitate the selection process and guarantee a more satisfactory experience for the client.

Identify the options that are most aligned with the customer's needs and that offer differentiated benefits. Select those that are representative and that cover the main characteristics or variants of the product or service that you are offering.

When presenting options to the client, it is important to identify those that best suit their needs and that offer differentiated benefits. This implies selecting representative options that cover the main characteristics or variants of the product or service that is being offered.

For example, if you are selling mobile phones, instead of presenting a wide range of models, you can identify those that align with the specific needs of the customer. If the customer values a high-quality camera, you can highlight models with excellent image resolution and advanced photography features. If the customer prioritizes battery life, you can focus on models with longer autonomy. By offering options that are tailored to the customer's needs and preferences, you increase the chances of closing the sale.

In the case of the sale of vacation packages, instead of presenting an endless list of destinations and accommodation options, it is advisable to select representative options that offer differentiated benefits. For example, if the client is looking for a luxury experience, you can offer packages at five-star resorts with exclusive services. If the customer prefers outdoor adventures, you can highlight options that include activities like hiking or diving. By presenting options that cover different interests and preferences, you facilitate the customer's choice process and increase the chances of closing the sale.

In the case of business consulting services, instead of offering a single standard package, it is advisable to tailor the options to the specific needs of each client. For example, if a client needs advice on digital marketing strategy, you can offer a package that includes market analysis, advertising campaign development, and results monitoring. If another client requires assistance in optimizing internal processes, you can offer a package that includes efficiency analysis, workflow design, and staff training. By presenting personalized options tailored to the individual needs of each client, you demonstrate your ability to provide specific solutions and increase the chances of closing the sale.

By carefully identifying and selecting options that fit customer needs and offer differentiated benefits, you will be able to present a more focused and relevant offer. This will increase the customer's perception of value and facilitate decision-making, thus favoring the closing of the sale. The proper selection and presentation of options that align with customer needs and offer differentiated benefits can contribute to a successful close in several ways.

First, by presenting options that are directly related to customer needs and preferences, you demonstrate a deep understanding of their requirements and show genuine interest in meeting their expectations. This builds trust and establishes a stronger connection between the seller and the customer, which is critical to closing the sale.

In addition, offering options that offer differentiated benefits allows you to highlight the unique and attractive aspects of each option. This helps to effectively communicate the value of the product or service and how it can solve problems or meet customer needs. By highlighting the specific benefits that each option provides, you are providing a strong argument that convinces the customer that making a favorable decision is the best option.

Likewise, limiting the number of options available avoids overwhelming the customer and facilitates decision making. Presenting a long list of options can confuse the customer and make them feel indecisive. Instead, by offering a manageable number of representative options, you give the customer the opportunity to evaluate each one more effectively and make an informed decision.

By selecting options that fit the customer's needs and preferences, you are personalizing the shopping experience. This shows the customer that you are willing to accommodate their individual needs and that you value their opinion. By feeling listened to and cared for, the customer feels more inclined to make the purchase and establish a lasting relationship with you as a seller.

Careful selection of options and their appropriate presentation, based on customer needs and preferences, helps establish a stronger connection, communicates the value of the product or service effectively, facilitates decision-making, and personalizes the shopping experience. All of this contributes to a successful close by building trust, meeting customer needs, and demonstrating the salesperson's commitment to customer satisfaction.

- *highlight the differences.*

When presenting the options, be sure to highlight the key differences between them, such as features, benefits, and pricing. This will help the client to evaluate the options and choose the one that best suits their needs.

Highlighting the differences between the options is a crucial aspect in guiding the client in his decision making and achieving a successful sales closure. When presenting the different options, it is important to highlight the distinctive features, the unique benefits and the prices associated with each of them.

By highlighting the key differences, you are providing relevant information that allows the customer to more accurately evaluate the options and make an informed decision.

By highlighting the distinctive features of each option, you are providing the customer with detailed information about the advantages and disadvantages of each. This allows you to better evaluate the options and make an informed decision.

When you identify the unique characteristics of each option, you are highlighting the aspects that differentiate them from each other. In the mobile phone example, you might mention that one option has a higher resolution camera, which means the customer will be able to capture exceptional quality photos and videos. On the other hand, you can highlight that another option has a greater storage capacity, which will allow the client to save more applications, files and multimedia on their device.

When communicating these distinctive features, it is important to explain how they translate into concrete benefits for the customer. For example, you can mention that a higher resolution camera will allow the client to capture sharp and detailed memories, which is ideal for those interested in photography or who want to have high quality images to share on social networks. Similarly, highlighting that an option has a higher storage capacity means that the customer will be able to have more apps, music, photos and videos on their device without worrying about running out of space.

It is essential that these distinctive characteristics are aligned with the needs and preferences of the client. Therefore, before highlighting the features, it is important to understand the expectations and requirements of the customer. This will allow you to focus your message on those aspects that really interest you and that can make a difference in your user experience.

Also, it is important to note that distinctive features are not just limited to technical aspects. They can also include aspects related to design, durability, ergonomics or any other characteristic that may be relevant to the client.

By communicating the distinctive features of each option, you are helping the customer understand the advantages and disadvantages of each. This allows you to evaluate the options more accurately and make an informed decision. Remember that it is important to highlight the specific benefits that these features provide and tailor your message to the customer's needs and preferences.

By highlighting the specific benefits of each option, you are providing the customer with a clear understanding of how each option can uniquely meet their needs or solve their problems. To achieve this, it is important to follow a few key steps. You must identify the needs and problems of the client. This involves asking open-ended questions and listening carefully to their answers to understand what they are looking for. For example, if you're selling home security systems, you might ask about their security concerns and what matters most to them.

Once you've identified their needs, you can relate the specific benefits of each option to those particular needs. For example, if an option offers advanced motion detection, you can highlight how this provides greater protection against intruders. If another option has high-resolution cameras, you can mention how this provides more detailed surveillance. By matching specific benefits to specific customer needs, you help them visualize how each option can enhance their experience.

By highlighting the specific benefits of each option and relating them to customer needs, you are demonstrating the value that your product or service can provide. This creates a link between what the customer is looking for and what you are offering, generating a sense of relevance and satisfaction.

By offering examples and testimonials from satisfied customers, you're backing up your claims with social proof, which increases customer confidence in the quality and effectiveness of your options. Also, by allowing the customer to experience the benefits through demos or trials, you are generating a hands-on experience that reinforces the perception of value and usefulness.

These strategies help eliminate doubts and objections that the client may have, since you provide them with clear and specific information about how your product or service can improve their situation. By highlighting the differences between the options and focusing on the relevant benefits, you are facilitating decision making and guiding the customer towards the most suitable option for them.

Ultimately, by using these closing techniques, you are building trust and showing a genuine commitment to the customer's needs. This strengthens the relationship and increases the chances of a successful closing. By offering a personalized and compelling experience, you are maximizing the chances of converting a prospect into a satisfied customer.

- ***Communicate the price***

The concept of prices and value is essential for closing an effective sale. By clearly communicating the price of each option and highlighting the value it offers in relation to that price, you are providing important information to the customer so that they can evaluate and compare the different alternatives.

When you present the price of an option, it is essential to do so transparently and without hiding information. This builds customer trust and shows your honesty as a seller. In addition, by highlighting the value that is obtained for that price, you are helping the customer to understand the advantages and benefits that they will receive when making the purchase.

In this sense, it is important to highlight the specific elements that make each option valuable and attractive. You can focus on unique features, additional benefits, or add-on services that are included in the price. For example, if you're selling vacation packages, you might highlight that an option includes free airport transportation, access to exclusive recreational activities, or personalized concierge services. By doing so, you are demonstrating to the customer that the price paid translates into tangible added value.

The impact of effectively communicating price and value at the close of the sale is significant. By highlighting the value for money invested, you are influencing the customer's perception of the cost-benefit ratio. If the customer perceives that they are getting more benefits and value for what they are paying for, they are more likely to be motivated to make the purchase decision.

Likewise, by clearly communicating price and value, you are helping the customer to justify their investment and feel more secure in their choice.

By understanding what they will get for their money, the customer will feel more confident and comfortable making the purchase.

Clear communication of price and value is essential to closing the sale. By highlighting the value for money paid and showing how each option offers unique and differentiated benefits, you are providing the customer with the information they need to make an informed decision. This influences the client's perception of the value of your offer and increases the chances of a successful closing.

- *Help with decision making*

The concept of help in decision making is essential in the process of closing a sale. If a customer shows indecision or doubts between the different options presented, as a seller, you have the opportunity to provide additional support and guide them towards the best choice.

An effective way to help the client in his decision making is to provide additional advice. You can provide additional information about the options, highlighting their key features and benefits, as well as clarify any questions or concerns the customer may have. This demonstrates your knowledge about the product or service, as well as your willingness to help the customer make the best decision for their needs.

In addition, you can use strategic questioning techniques to guide the client in his decision process. By asking pertinent and relevant questions, you can help the client to reflect on their needs and priorities, allowing them to assess which option best suits their requirements. For example, you could ask, "What are the most important things you look for in a product/service?" or "What specific features are you most interested in?" These questions help focus the client's attention on the aspects that are relevant to their decision and allow them to evaluate the options more objectively.

By providing additional advice and asking strategic questions, you are showing your commitment to helping the client make an informed and satisfying decision. This not only demonstrates your experience and knowledge in the field of sales, but also your service attitude towards the customer. By doing so, you are building a relationship of trust and establishing a solid foundation for closing the sale.

It is important to note that when providing decision support, you must be impartial and focus on the client's best interests. Avoid being overly persuasive or biasing the decision towards a specific option without taking into account the customer's needs and preferences. The goal is to provide information and guidance that empowers the client to make the best decision for themselves.

The concept of decision support has a significant impact on closing the sale. By providing additional advice and guiding the customer towards the best option, you are building trust and generating a higher level of satisfaction in their purchase process. This, in turn, can increase the chances of successfully closing the sale.

When the customer feels supported and understood, they are more likely to feel confident in their decision and willing to commit to the purchase. By providing additional information and clarifying their doubts, you are removing barriers that could hinder the closing of the sale. At the same time, you are demonstrating your experience and knowledge, which increases your credibility as a seller.

Also, by asking strategic questions, you are helping the client to assess their needs and priorities. By reflecting on what they are really looking for, the client can make a more informed decision aligned with their objectives. This reduces indecision and eases the process of closing the sale.

Help in decision making also shows your willingness to serve the customer and your commitment to finding the best solution for their needs. This creates a stronger connection between you and the client, which can lead to long-term business relationships and potential referrals from other clients.

By providing help in decision making, you are removing barriers, building trust and facilitating the customer's decision making. This increases the chances of achieving a successful closing, since the client will feel more secure and satisfied with their choice. At the same time, you are laying a solid foundation for future business relationships and business opportunities.

Closure by assumption

Closing by assumption is a sales technique in which the seller starts from the premise that the customer has already made the decision to make the purchase. Instead of directly asking the customer if they are ready to buy, the salesperson assumes the answer is yes and moves towards closing the sale.

This technique is based on the idea that by showing confidence and acting as if the sale is already secured, the closer can influence the customer's mindset and make the closing process easier. By avoiding direct questions about the purchase decision, possible objections or doubts that could arise in the customer's mind are avoided.

When applying the closing by assumption, the seller uses a language and tone of voice that convey confidence and certainty that the customer has made the decision to buy. Instead of asking direct questions about purchase intent, the salesperson makes statements that assume the sale will go through.

By using this approach, the closer avoids putting the customer in an awkward position by directly asking if they are ready to buy. Instead, use phrases that presuppose the purchase and allow the customer to confirm or clarify the details.

An example of language used in the assumption close might be: "So when would you like to receive your order?" This statement assumes that the customer is ready to make the purchase and only logistical details, such as the delivery date, remain to be determined.

Another example could be: "I see that this product is perfectly suited to your needs. What is your delivery address?". With this statement, the seller assumes that the customer has decided to buy and only needs to provide the information necessary to complete the transaction.

The tone of voice also plays an important role in closing by assumption. The salesperson should use a confident, friendly, and convincing tone. You must convey confidence in the customer's decision and in the ability of the product or service to meet their needs.

It is important to note that the assumption closure must be used appropriately and sensitively. Not all customers will be ready to make a purchase decision at that point, and some may need more information or time to consider their choice. The salesperson must be attentive to the signals and responses of the customer to adapt their approach and provide the best possible shopping experience.

Closing by assumption involves using a language and tone of voice that presupposes the sale and allows the customer to confirm his decision. This avoids direct questions and puts the client in a more comfortable position. However, it is important to use this technique sensitively and to adapt to the individual needs of each client.

Although closing by assumption can be an effective technique to facilitate the sales process, it is essential to keep in mind that not all clients will be ready to make an immediate decision. Some customers may express resistance, indecision, or a need for more time to consider their purchase. In these cases, it is essential that the seller is sensitive to these signals and is willing to adapt his approach.

When a customer clearly expresses that they have not made a purchase decision or shows resistance, it is essential that the closer avoid being pushy or pressuring the customer into a sale. Instead, it is important to adopt an attitude of empathy and understanding towards concerns or doubts that may arise.

First, the closer must demonstrate active listening and pay attention to the concerns expressed by the customer. It is important to allow the client to feel heard and understood by giving them the opportunity to express their concerns and questions without feeling pressured.

Once the customer has expressed his concerns, the closer must show understanding and empathy towards his prospect. Acknowledging and validating customer concerns will help build trust and establish a trusting relationship. This involves avoiding defensive responses or attempts to convince the client that their concerns are unfounded.

Instead of dwelling on the sale, the closer can focus on providing additional information or clarification that addresses the customer's concerns. This may mean offering testimonials from other satisfied customers who have faced similar situations, providing additional data about the product or service that demonstrates its quality and benefits, or even offering guarantees or return policies to give the customer peace of mind.

It is important to remember that client resistance can arise for a variety of reasons, such as lack of information, uncertainty, or the need to consider other options. Therefore, the salesperson must adapt to the situation and show patience and willingness to help the customer in his decision-making process.

When a customer expresses resistance or has not made a purchase decision, the closer should avoid being pushy and instead show empathy and understanding toward the customer's concerns. Providing additional information, testimonials, and clarification can help address concerns and build customer trust. The key lies in building a relationship of trust based on understanding and willingness to help the client make an informed and satisfactory decision.

Instead of using the assumption close, the closer can shift their focus to other closing techniques or address customer objections. For example, you can use the question-closing technique to dig further into the customer's concerns and offer solutions or additional clarification. You can also use the closing by testimonials, presenting successful cases or testimonials from satisfied customers that can generate confidence in the purchase decision. It is crucial that the closer watch for signs of resistance or indecision on the part of the customer. In these cases, it's important to adapt your approach, show empathy, and use other closing techniques or address customer objections appropriately. The key to a successful closing is to provide a personalized sales experience tailored to the individual needs of each client.

Emergency closure

Urgent closing is a sales technique that harnesses customer psychology to drive buying decisions quickly. It is based on the premise that when a situation of urgency or shortage occurs, the client feels more motivated to act to take advantage of the opportunity before it runs out.

One of the most common ways to enforce the lockout is by setting a deadline for a special promotion. For example, you can announce that a discount or special offer will only be available for a limited time, creating a sense of urgency for the customer to take action before the opportunity to save money or take advantage of the promotion runs out.

Another way to use the emergency closing is by offering discounts or additional benefits for a limited time. For example, an additional discount can be offered to the first customers to make a purchase, creating an incentive for the customer to make a quick decision and take advantage of the exclusive offer. In addition, highlighting the limited availability of a product or service can also create urgency for the customer.

To create a sense of scarcity or limitation in your emergency closing, there are several effective strategies you can use. One is to highlight the limited number of products available, informing the customer of the exact number of units remaining or using phrases such as "available only while supplies last." This creates the feeling that the product is highly desirable and can sell out quickly.

Another strategy is to set a limited time for the promotion or special discount. By clearly communicating a deadline, you create a sense of urgency in the customer, who knows that after that date they will lose the opportunity to get the offer. It is important to highlight the temporality and remind the client about the proximity of the deadline.

You can also use exclusivity as a way to create scarcity. By making the customer feel privileged by having access to an exclusive or limited offer, you will increase their interest and the feeling that they are taking advantage of a unique opportunity. You can mention that the offer is available only to certain customers or to a select group.

An effective strategy to generate urgency in customer decision making is to tie the offer to a special event or season. This technique is commonly used in the sales arena to take advantage of the feeling of exclusivity and limited opportunity associated with certain times of the year or specific events.

Take, for example, a salesperson who wants to promote a special offer on electronics. In this case, they could take advantage of an event like Black Friday, which is a date recognized worldwide for its discounts and offers on products. The seller could run a promotion that offers exclusive prices on a selection of electronic products for a limited period, for example, from November 23 to 26.

By tying the sale to Black Friday, the seller creates a sense of temporary urgency. Customers know that only during those days will they have the opportunity to access special prices on electronic products, which motivates them to make a quick decision. This strategy is based on the psychological principle of scarcity, since the perception is created that the offer is limited and exclusive for that particular event.

The seller could communicate this promotion through various channels, such as social networks, emails to their customer base and advertisements in their physical store. In addition, they could highlight the benefits of buying high-quality electronics at reduced prices during Black Friday, such as financial savings and the opportunity to obtain cutting-edge technology at more affordable prices.

By using this strategy, the seller not only generates urgency in customers' decision making, but also associates it with an event that is recognized and expected by consumers. This strengthens the emotional connection with the seller and creates a sense of trust and satisfaction in customers knowing that they are taking advantage of a special offer during a special time.

Remember that when using these strategies, it is essential to be honest and transparent. The idea is to create a feeling of real or temporary scarcity to motivate the client to make a quick decision, but always providing accurate information and fulfilling the promises made. This will help build trust and maintain a strong long-term customer relationship. Urgent closing can be an effective technique to expedite the sales process, but it is important to use it with integrity and transparency. It is essential to provide truthful information and support the urgency presented with a valid reason, whether it is due to limited availability, a temporary offer or exclusive benefits.

It is essential to provide truthful and relevant information that supports the need to act immediately. This involves presenting strong arguments and hard data that demonstrate the benefits and advantages of making an early decision. The idea is not to create a false sense of urgency based on misleading information, but to provide strong arguments that help the client understand why it is beneficial to act quickly.

The generation of urgency must be aligned with the needs and interests of the client, offering solutions that really satisfy their requirements. This involves actively listening to the customer, understanding their concerns, and tailoring communication in a personalized way.

It is crucial to respect the client's limits and time. While you want to create a sense of urgency, it's also important to recognize that each person has their own pace and decision-making process. Pushing or forcing a customer beyond their limits can negatively impact the business relationship in the long run.

Using urgency generation techniques in an ethical and genuine way implies providing truthful and relevant information, adapting to the individual needs of the client and respecting their limits and times. By doing so, a relationship of trust is established and the chances of the client making informed and mutually beneficial decisions are maximized.

Closing for questions

Question closing is a powerful technique used in sales to help the customer come to the conclusion that the product or service offered meets their needs or desires. Instead of forcing the sale directly, the closer uses strategic questions to guide the customer toward a favorable buying decision.

The key to this technique lies in formulating questions that direct the customer's attention to the most relevant benefits and characteristics of the product or service. These questions are designed to arouse the interest and reflection of the client, allowing him to realize for himself that the solution offered is the right one to meet his needs.

For example, suppose a salesperson is promoting an online training program. Instead of saying outright, "This training program is perfect for you," the closer might ask questions like:

- Would you like to have access to a training program that suits your schedule and lifestyle?
- Have you been looking for a convenient way to stay fit and achieve your health goals?
- Would you be interested in having a program that includes personalized follow-up and constant support?

These questions are designed to engage the client's attention and direct it toward the key benefits of the online training program, such as flexibility, convenience, and personalized support. As the customer reflects on these questions, he realizes that the product offered meets his needs and desires.

It is important to note that question closing is not about manipulating the customer, but about guiding them towards an informed decision. Questions must be genuine and relevant, based on a thorough understanding of the customer's needs and an understanding of how the product or service can help them.

This question-closing technique allows the closer to actively involve the customer in the sales process and gives them the opportunity to make an informed decision. Doing so establishes greater trust and increases the likelihood of successfully closing the sale.

The approach of strategic questions for closing sales in the new times is based on adapting to the changing needs and preferences of customers, as well as taking advantage of available tools and technologies. This new approach can be call "QUADS" (Questions for Understanding, Assessing, Discovering, and Suggesting).

1. Questions to understand.
Rather than simply gathering basic information about the client's situation, understanding questions focus on deeply understanding the client's goals, challenges, and values. These questions seek to know your long-term vision and the motivations behind your decisions.

By using insight questions to close the sale, the salesperson seeks to go beyond simply gathering superficial data. The goal is to fully understand the client's goals, challenges, and values in order to offer a solution that aligns with their long-term needs and desires.

During this stage, the salesperson should ask open-ended, probing questions that invite the customer to share relevant information about their business goals, concerns, aspirations, and what they truly value in a solution. These questions should be carefully designed to encourage deep and meaningful conversation, allowing the closer to get inside the customer's mind and gain a fuller picture of their situation.

An example of a question to understand at closing might be: "What are the biggest challenges your business is currently facing, and how do you think a solution like ours could help you overcome them?" This question allows the salesperson to understand the customer's specific concerns and difficulties, as well as giving him the opportunity to express his expectations and needs.

By thoroughly understanding the customer's goals, challenges, and values, the salesperson can personalize their approach and present a compelling proposition that demonstrates how their offer can help achieve the desired results. This deep understanding also helps establish a stronger and more trusting connection with the customer, increasing the chances of a successful close.

2. Questions to evaluate.
These questions are focused on helping the client assess the potential benefits and results of the offered solution. The evaluation criteria are explored and key aspects that demonstrate how the offer can meet those criteria are highlighted.

The use of questions to evaluate during the closing process of the sale is essential to help the client understand and appreciate the benefits and results that can be obtained by choosing the solution that is offered. These questions focus on exploring the customer's evaluation criteria and highlighting key aspects that demonstrate how the offer effectively meets those criteria.

An effective strategy is to inquire about the client's success criteria, asking what are the results or achievements that they would consider as signs of success when implementing the solution. This helps the customer to reflect on their expectations and allows the seller to highlight how the offer can meet those specific criteria.

Also, asking about the customer's previous experiences with similar solutions is another valuable tactic. This allows the seller to understand what aspects were most relevant to the customer in the past and how they can be applied to the current offer. You can also identify areas for improvement and highlight how the new solution addresses those concerns.

Exploring competitive advantages is another key technique. The closer may ask the customer which features or benefits they value most when comparing different options. This helps identify the strengths of the offer and allows you to highlight how it outperforms the competition in those key aspects.

Finally, requesting examples or success stories is a powerful strategy. The seller may ask the customer to share specific examples of situations in which the benefits offered would be especially relevant. This helps the client to visualize how the solution can be applied to their own context and provides a solid basis for decision making.

Evaluation questions allow the salesperson to guide the customer through a reflective and analytical process, helping him to understand and appreciate the benefits and results that can be obtained by choosing the proposed solution. By tailoring these questions to the customer's needs and preferences, the closer can build greater confidence and motivation to successfully close the sale.

3. Questions to discover.
Rather than assuming customer needs, discovery questions focus on fostering a collaborative conversation to fully explore customer issues, challenges, and opportunities. These questions seek to uncover new perspectives and trigger innovative ideas that can lead to a more effective solution.

Questions to discover at the close of the sale are an essential tool to go beyond the assumptions and dig deeper into the problems, challenges and opportunities of the client. Rather than assuming the client's needs, these questions foster a collaborative conversation that allows one to fully explore the client's unique situations and seek effective solutions.

When using this technique, the closer focuses on asking open-ended, provocative questions that invite the customer to share more information about their situation. Some examples of questions to discover could be: "What are the main challenges you are currently facing in your business/personal life?" or "How are these challenges impacting your goals and objectives?"

The goal of these questions is to open up a deeper conversation and allow the closer to gain valuable insight into the customer's needs and wants. By actively listening to the responses, the salesperson can uncover new insights and spark innovative ideas that could lead to a more effective and customer-friendly solution.

In addition to eliciting information, discovery questions also create an environment of trust and collaboration. The customer feels valued and understood, which strengthens the relationship between the seller and the customer. By showing a genuine interest in understanding the customer's needs and challenges, the salesperson demonstrates his commitment and willingness to find the best solution.

The result of using discovery questions is the generation of a greater connection with the customer, the identification of hidden opportunities and the presentation of a personalized value proposition. By tailoring the offer based on the responses, the salesperson shows the customer that they care about their success and are willing to work together to find the best solution.

Uncovering closing questions are a powerful strategy for understanding customer needs, building trust, and presenting an offer that effectively addresses specific customer challenges and needs. By employing this technique, salespeople can achieve a higher success rate in closing sales and establish lasting and satisfying relationships with customers.

4. Questions to suggest.
These questions focus on presenting specific ideas, solutions, and recommendations to the client. They are based on the prior understanding gained through the questions above and are tailored to the individual needs and preferences of the client. These questions are intended to guide the customer towards an informed purchase decision and help them to visualize how the offer can solve their problems or satisfy their needs.

In the closing stage of the sale, the questions to suggest play a fundamental role. Having thoroughly understood the customer's needs, wants, and challenges through the questions above, the salesperson is prepared to present specific ideas, solutions, and recommendations that align with those needs.

These questions are based on information collected during the exploration stage and are tailored to individual customer preferences. The goal is to offer options that resonate with them and allow them to visualize how the offer can effectively solve their problems or meet their needs.

During the closing process, the closer can use questions that lead the customer to reflect and consider the advantages of the offer. Some examples could be:

> - *"Given what we've discussed so far and considering your goals, would you consider it useful to have a solution that can streamline your processes and save you time?"*
>
> - *"Based on our conversation above and understanding your specific needs, would you be interested in learning how our services can help you reduce operating costs and improve the efficiency of your business?"*
>
> - *"Given your long-term goals and considering the competition in the market, would you like to explore how our offering can give you a competitive advantage and contribute to the growth of your company?"*

These questions help guide the customer toward an informed buying decision by highlighting the specific benefits and results the offer can bring them. Additionally, by customizing suggestions to individual needs and preferences, a higher level of connection and relevance is created for the customer.

It's critical that the salesperson back up their suggestions with relevant examples, case studies, or testimonials from satisfied customers. Doing so builds trust and gives the customer the confidence to make an informed buying decision. These prompting questions should not be manipulative or misleading, but rather be authentic and genuine, based on a real understanding of the client and their particular situation.

To train in the QUADS approach to closing sales, the salesperson can follow several key steps. First of all, it is important to thoroughly study and understand the fundamental principles and concepts of the QUADS approach. This involves spending time reading and studying relevant material, such as books and articles, to gain a solid understanding of how to apply this approach in real sales situations.

Also, practice is essential. The salesperson can participate in role- play exercises that simulate sales situations, which will allow them to put the QUADS approach into practice and develop skills in asking quality questions, actively listening to customer responses, and adapting solutions based on their needs. . Practicing with colleagues or mentors and receiving constructive feedback is essential to improving and honing skills.

Observing and learning from experienced salespeople is another valuable strategy. Taking the opportunity to accompany more experienced salespeople on customer visits, participate in joint sales meetings, or even watch recordings of successful interactions can provide valuable practical lessons. Observing how relevant questions are asked, how attentively the customer is listened to, and how sales are successfully closed can provide practical guidance for the salesperson's own performance.

Feedback is critical to salesperson growth and development. Seeking feedback from both customers and colleagues or mentors allows you to assess performance and gain insight into areas for improvement. Feedback can provide valuable insights on how to improve question formulation, tailor solutions, and close sales effectively. Based on the feedback received, the salesperson can make any necessary adjustments in their approach and skills.

Lastly, it is important to stay current and learn from best practices in the field of sales. This means keeping up with the latest trends, tools, and techniques by reading relevant books, subscribing to specialized blogs or podcasts, attending conferences, and participating in training courses. Keeping up with current knowledge allows the seller to enrich the QUADS approach and be prepared to adapt to changing customer needs.

Training in the QUADS approach to closing deals requires in-depth study, diligent practice, observing and learning from experienced salespeople, constructive feedback, and the constant search for up-to-date knowledge. By following these steps, the salesperson will be better equipped to master the QUADS approach and use it effectively in their interactions with customers.

This QUADS approach emphasizes the importance of asking strategic questions and focusing on customer understanding and collaboration. By adapting to changing times, sellers can use this methodology to generate a greater connection with customers, provide personalized solutions and achieve successful sales closures.

Conclusion

Throughout the book, various strategies and practical tips are presented to help salespeople achieve success in their sales activities.

Emphasis was placed on the critical importance of building strong customer relationships. It was highlighted that strong relationships are the foundation for building a loyal and satisfied customer base. This means focusing not just on closing sales, but on genuinely understanding customer needs, wants, and challenges.

To achieve this, the need to develop effective communication skills was highlighted. This implies the ability to clearly convey the benefits and features of products or services, as well as the ability to actively listen to customers to understand their specific needs. The importance of avoiding one-way communication and focusing on establishing a meaningful dialogue with customers, enabling a deeper understanding of their needs, was emphasized.

In addition, the importance of active listening and empathy towards customers was discussed. This involves being able to read between the lines, grasping underlying concerns, and understanding customer emotions. By demonstrating empathy, salespeople can establish a deeper connection with customers, building trust and loyalty.

It was underscored that offering customized solutions is key to building strong customer relationships. Each client has unique needs and therefore it is essential to tailor solutions to their particular circumstances. This involves thoroughly understanding the products or services offered and being able to present them in a way that highlights how they align with the customer's needs and goals. Personalization creates additional value and shows the customer that the seller is committed to their success and satisfaction.

The importance of maintaining a positive and persevering mentality in the sales process was highlighted. Successful salespeople understand that they will face challenges and rejection on their way, but they see it as part of the process and are not easily discouraged. Instead of giving up, they use each obstacle as an opportunity to learn, grow, and improve. They maintain an optimistic attitude, adapt to changing circumstances, and seek creative solutions to overcome challenges that arise.

Successful salespeople understand that building lasting relationships and building trust are critical to long-term success. Therefore, vendors were encouraged to maintain high ethical standards in all of their interactions with customers. The importance of avoiding deceptive or manipulative practices that could damage the reputation and trust of the sales profession was highlighted. Instead, the importance of being transparent, honest and ethical in all business transactions and decisions was emphasized.

To be a successful seller, it is essential to know your ideal client thoroughly. Spend time understanding their needs, wants, and concerns in order to tailor your products or services effectively. Also, develop strong communication skills to express yourself clearly, persuasively, and empathetically. Listen carefully to your customers and use non-verbal communication techniques to establish a strong connection with them.

Instead of focusing solely on selling, work on building strong, long-term relationships. Establish trust and credibility with your customers through excellent customer service and consistent follow-up. Be proactive in your sales approach, search for leads and offer solutions before they ask for them.

Learn from rejections and obstacles you may encounter along the way. Use them as learning opportunities to improve your sales skills and adjust your approach. Don't be discouraged by rejections, but use those moments as an impetus to keep going and grow.

Become an expert in your industry. Spend time staying up to date on related trends, products and services. This will give you confidence and allow you to offer added value to your customers, making you a trusted and knowledgeable resource.

Set clear, measurable goals to stay focused and motivated. Break your goals into smaller objectives and establish an action plan to achieve them. Also, be flexible and adaptable, as the world of sales is constantly changing. Learn to quickly adjust to new situations and challenges, and look for creative solutions.

Take the opportunity to learn from other successful sellers. Observe and study their techniques and approaches. Participate in training programs, read sales books, and seek mentoring from experienced professionals. Never stop learning and constantly seek opportunities for professional growth and development.

Remember that being a successful salesperson requires dedication, perseverance, and a positive attitude. Apply these tips consistently and you'll be well on your way to reaching your sales goals. Stay motivated and enthusiastic, and remember that every customer interaction is an opportunity to learn and grow.

In general, the book provides a complete and practical vision of the world of sales, offering salespeople the necessary tools to achieve success and obtain outstanding results in their sales activities.

Recommended reading

These books cover a variety of sales approaches and strategies, from the psychology of persuasion to practical closing techniques. Each one of them offers a unique and valuable perspective for those who want to improve their skills and achieve success in the world of sales.

- "The Art of Persuasion: Strategies to Convince and Sell" - Robert Cialdini.
- "How to Win Friends and Influence People" - Dale Carnegie.
- "The World's Greatest Salesman" - Og Mandino
- "The 7 Habits of Highly Effective People" - Stephen R. Covey
- "Influencers: The Power to Change Anything" - Kerry Patterson
- "Pitch Anything: An Innovative Method for Presenting, Persuading, and Winning the Deal" - Oren Klaff
- "The Little Book of Big Sales" - Jeffrey Gitomer
- "The Seller of Dreams" - Augusto Cury
- "How to Win at Selling: 21 Proven Lessons for Closing Deals" - Brian Tracy
- "The Professional Sales" - Alejandro Hernández Yáñez
- "The Challenger Sale: Taking Control of the Customer Conversation" - Matthew Dixon and Brent Adamson
- "Effective Sales: Techniques and Methods to Sell Any Product or Service" - Jorge Muniain Gómez
- "Sales 3.0: How to Sell in Today's Environment" - Jürgen Klaric
- "Fanatical Prospecting: The Ultimate Guide to Opening Sales Conversations and Filling the Pipeline by Leveraging Social Selling, Telephone, Email, Text, and Cold Calling" - Jeb Blount
- "The Psychology of Selling: Increase Your Sales Faster and Easier Than You Ever Thought Possible" - Brian Tracy
- "Secrets of the Millionaire Mind" - T. Harv eker
- "The Sales Acceleration Formula: Using Data, Technology, and Inbound Selling to Go from $0 to $100 Million" - Mark Roberge
- "SPIN Selling " - Neil Rackham
- "The Perfect Close: Effective Techniques for Closing Sales" - James Muir

www.ingramcontent.com/pod-product-compliance
Lightning Source LLC
Chambersburg PA
CBHW070649220526
45466CB00001B/365